HIT Your Mark

&

Live The Life You Love

Mark Jarema

HIT Your Mark

ISBN-13: 978-0-578-20748-3

Printed in by 48HrBooks (www.48HrBooks.com)

Dedication

THIS BOOK IS dedicated in loving memory of my sister Melanie. She was a dreamer who was not afraid to be different. She believed in me. She inspired me. She was an imperfect perfect sister, whom I loved. She represented the words of Ralph Waldo Emerson: "Do not go where the path may lead, go instead where there is no path and leave a trail."

Table of Contents

Foreword

I AM REALLY excited about this book! Not only because Mark Jarema is my protegé, but also because I consider Mark a brother from another mother. We are kindred spirits. Mark is also the conqueror of what I fondly refer to as the little 'c'. I believe it's important to have as many voices of hope and triumph as possible. People often have dreams and aspirations but no real clues as to how they can change their circumstances. There is an old saying: "People aiming at nothing usually hit nothing dead on the head." This book gives you simple, concise steps for how to "Hit Your Mark." It is a must read! It is important to learn from those who have endured and succeeded. My favorite book, the Bible, tells us we will all face the fiery furnaces of this world. We all face challenges and have obstacles to overcome on this journey that we call life. You can allow life to make you bitter or life can make you better! Mark Jarema is a shining example of what courage looks like in the face of adversity. Each day we have a choice to make when we wake up. You can choose to be a volunteer victim or choose to face life's challenges and live victoriously! Mark shares advice for doing so from personal life experience. He explains how to develop mastery of self by holding yourself accountable and reinventing yourself with kick-butt determination to hit your mark. Success is a journey, not a destination, whether you are an entrepreneur, whether you're trying to get out of a dead-end job, or you're just searching for some direction. Do you want to know how to get your business or life jumpstarted??? I strongly recommend that you read this book, "Hit your Mark." In order to make lasting impact on the planet, this will take courage, commitment and a game plan. I believe that success leaves clues. This book provides some of those clues on how to tap into your greatness! If you want to live the dream, you have to pay the dues. Mark shares how you can make a difference in the world and live your best life ever, despite your circumstances. Always remember that you have something special. You have greatness within you! That's my story and I am sticking to it.

Mamie Brown's baby boy,

Les Brown

Introduction

SUCCESS IS NOT easy, but it's worth the effort. For several years, I have studied the art of success—and yes, it *is* an art. I have studied the leaders whom I have worked with, admired, and respected. I have also studied many people who have changed the world. I went on a journey to find the attributes successful people have. What makes them tick? What makes them different?

So, why should you read this book? Because I have done some of the homework for you. I have tried to figure out why those who graduate from the best schools, are highly intelligent, and were raised by good families often struggle to achieve their goals and why some with no formal education who were raised with all the chips stacked against them achieve great success. Then, there are those somewhere in the middle. The people I have found to be in the upper tier of life understand and implement what is between the covers of this book. I have given over a couple thousand seminars to tens of thousands of people in twenty-two countries. I am an instructor, speaker, and coach, but I am also a student who learned from those who have achieved happiness and success.

I'm one of the most optimistic, positive people you will ever meet, but my tone in this book is direct. What I have learned is that to help people achieve the next level in their personal life or career, you must shake the tree—sometimes *really* hard—to get thoughts to fall and get people to do something different. There are "gloves-on" books and "gloves-off" books; this is a gloves-off book.

This book will cut through the noise and get to the point. When I started this book, a friend of mine told me in a discouraging way that hundreds of books on the same subject have already been written. I replied, "Yes, that's true, and I have read many of them—but they didn't connect with *me*." I have read a wall full of self-help books. The authors were knowledgeable, and the books had good information, but there are only a few books that truly moved me because I connected with the messenger. I'm hoping that this book finds its own set of people who connect to my message.

The other hope I have for this book is that it inspires you to do something different to achieve the next level in your life, either personally or professionally. You already have the knowledge; I want to nudge you to apply what you already know. Samuel Johnson said, "People need to be reminded more often than they need to be instructed." My intent is to *remind you of what you already know.* I want to bring the information from your subconscious mind to your conscious mind. I cannot change your life for you, but I can challenge you to reflect: to really think about yourself and your life. Then, deciding to make the necessary changes in your life is up to you.

This book is not the answer; in fact, no one book can tell you everything you need to know or what to do. Consider this book as a tool in your tool box to help you achieve greatness. The more tools you add to your toolbox, and the better you know how to use them, the better chance you have to *Hit Your Mark* and live the life you love.

Good luck with your journey. Let's get started…

Stop Conforming

ARE YOU LIVING your dreams, or making someone else's dreams come true? Everyone has a dream, but rarely do people pursue what they really want in life. We are conditioned at a very young age by conformers to conform to their ideas about life and live by their rules. For example, you must go to college, then work for 40 hours a week for 40 years to get the company pin or the fancy gold pen, and you will therefore be happy. Before we know it, weeks turn into months, months turn into years, and we end up only dreaming of our dreams, instead of taking action. We set goals and do what we think will make other people happy, instead of what makes us happy. The proof is in the pudding. Just ask anyone, if they had life to live over again, would they live it differently? Most people wouldn't hesitate to say *yes*!

If you take the first three letters of the word *conform*, you have *con*. *Con* means to deceive or use trickery. I believe conformers have conned themselves into living a life of complacency. We trick ourselves into thinking that external things will make us happy. People often tell me if they had more money, a different relationship, a promotion at work, a higher education, whatever it is, that they would be happier; but, the truth is that none of those external things will make you happier if you have not gone on the journey to discover yourself.

Many people are just going through the motions in life. They go to work and it's a charade. They are not being their true self, and their co-workers never get to know the *real* person, only seeing the mask. People are going to work day after day, making someone else rich while it's making them sick. In one Gallup poll, 87% of workers worldwide "are emotionally disconnected from their workplaces." Another way to look at it is that almost nine out of ten people have quit their jobs, they just haven't left yet.

We are in a very challenging time, and we must be willing to break the old mold of the past. Everything we read tells us the conformist message is not working. Divorce rates are over 50%. More than 71% of all Americans are living paycheck to paycheck. A whopping 24% of the country has more credit card debt than emergency savings. More than half of US wage earners made less than $30,000, which is just above poverty. In America, 10% of the population is diagnosed with depression, and the number increases every year by 20%. Five percent of the world population suffers from depression.

You deserve to be happy, not mentally stuck in a place called complacency. I see people every day walking the halls of their workplace as if their souls have been sucked out of them. They look like what they're going through, too. They act if they would rather be getting a root canal with no anesthetic than going to their job. They get to their desk and glance at a countdown calendar to retirement.

Conforming is like being a hamster running on a spinning wheel, chasing happiness and success but not getting any closer to your target. It is said that many people die at the age of 25 but they are not buried until the age of 85, because they have conformed and abandoned their dreams. Along their journey of life, they have lost their identity and have become like a ship adrift at sea. We think we can hide feeling lost, but the truth is, it shows up with our friends, family and in the workplace. If you fit this scenario, I can understand how you are feeling. I was one of you for many years.

To live your dream, you must become a nonconformer. A nonconformer thinks differently than conformers. Nonconformers are often looked upon as crazy, bold, and daring. They are the oddballs in life. Nonconformers understand they were not born to make a living, but to live their making. Be proud to be a nonconformer. Conformers will not understand you, because you are choosing not to go where society wants you to go. As a nonconformer, you will choose to go where *you* want to go.

Your time is now! You have a gift. You are not here by accident. Only you can make the choice to set yourself free from complacency. *It's time to water your dehydrated dreams.* You don't have to be great to get started, but you have to get started to be great. It's now or never; your dreams can't wait.

Become the Student

EARLY IN MY career, someone told me to never call yourself an expert because that opens the door for the snipers in life to target your expertise. They challenge you to prove yourself, hoping to reveal you really are not an expert. For the record, I'm not an expert. If we take it a step further, I don't even have a college degree.

Many of you can relate to some of the events in my life. I graduated high school and had a disc jockey business starting at the age of 14. I was making great money during my teens and learned how to run a small business. I wanted more of a challenge in life, so at the age of 19, I joined the Navy and served my country honorably for five years. After the service I ventured into the world of training, teaching people technology, professional development, and leadership.

At one point in my life, I was at the top of the mountain. I was a director leading a global training team, making well into the six figures, traveling the world, and had a ton of stock money. I purchased a house, renovated it into a model home, had new vehicles, ate out at nice restaurants almost every night, and was in love with a beautiful woman. Many, including myself, thought I had the perfect life.

And then, in a very short period, I tumbled from the top of the mountain to below sea level. It seemed like overnight that my life turned into a nightmare. I remember going to the ATM to withdraw $20 for food; my request was denied because I only had $2.22 in my account. My house was foreclosed on, and I lost my job. I was sued by a financial institution for an unpaid loan, I was diagnosed with a unique type of cancer, and my girlfriend left me.

I became a volunteer victim. I was blaming everyone and complaining about everything as to why my life suddenly sucked. I even blamed God. Have you ever had a moment when life knocked you on your backside and you blamed God? I didn't want to take responsibility for my life. I mentally moved into victimhood. I let my struggles become my standards.

I was raised in an excellent family. I could not have asked for better parents. I am proud to be their son. I could have asked them for help when I hit rock bottom, and they would have been there for me—but I was too embarrassed. Half my pain was feeling disgusted with choices that I had made, and the other half was being embarrassed about my failures.

I realized that up until my fall from success, I had a good life because I worked hard, good people helped me, I was in the right place at the right time, and I was lucky. I knew if I wanted to climb my way back to success and not just have a list of accomplishments, I needed to look at life differently. *If you change the way you look at things, the things you look at change.* I became a student of life.

Hit Your Mark

I HAVE DESIGNED a system that will empower you to *Hit Your Mark* in life. I use my first name, Mark, to emphasize four main pillars; Mastery, Accountability, Reinvention, and Kick-Butt Determination. There are many concepts under each pillar that provide ideas on how to take your life to the next level.

While I can share with you the concept of *Hit Your Mark*, you must be willing to take action and apply the concepts. The difference between what we know and don't know is not as great as the difference between what we know and what we are willing to do. As adults, we amass a lot of knowledge—but that doesn't necessarily mean we apply it to our lives. I would like for you to make the commitment now, before you read any further, that you will try to apply at least three things from this book. Don't do it for me; do it for *you*. You must be willing to do the things that other people won't today, to have the life they wish they had tomorrow.

I can't do it for you. You can't hire someone else to do you pushups, sing your songs, write your poems, or run your business—and I can't be with you every day to make sure you remain focused. I have worked with people who were highly intelligent but could not apply their intelligence to becoming successful. In the workplace, they looked like a zebra in the middle of a cow pasture. I have also worked with people that knew very little, but they applied what they knew with passion and reached a level in life few could imagine.

To live the life you love, you must have the knowledge and the determination to apply what you know. Knowledge and determination are the yin and yang of life. Simply having knowledge is not good enough. We are surrounded by knowledge, yet it isn't improving anyone's life at a faster rate. If I were to ask you if eating healthy and exercising is important, I know you would tell me yes. Of course you would! Your health is everything. If you don't have your health, then other things don't matter. Now, be honest; if you think health is important, do you eat healthy and exercise daily? I'm willing to bet you don't; if you do, congratulations, you are in the minority. If you don't eat healthy or exercise daily, then why not? I will guarantee it isn't because you don't have the knowledge. You know how to walk every day for 20 minutes. You know the difference between a salad and a doughnut. The challenge is applying the knowledge, using what you already know. It's the same thing for achieving greatness in your life; you already have the knowledge, but you must decide to act on it.

Those who are living their dreams are action-oriented. They don't just talk the talk; they walk the walk. Actions speak louder than words, and successful people practice what they preach. They walk it like they talk it. Only you can decide to take action on the knowledge you already have, or that you will learn from *Hit Your Mark*. It's going to take work. *Hard* work. We all want the prize, but do not want to pay the price. I trust that you will be different and are ready to work for it. One of my favorite Les Brown quotes is: "Do what is easy and your life will be hard. Do what is hard and your life will become easy." The concepts in this book are easy; it's the application that is difficult. It should be difficult. Easy is not an option. If it was easy, then success would lose its value. Success is a club, and to receive a membership, you must earn your way.

Success is challenging; therefore, it separates those who really want to put in the effort and work to achieve big results in their personal or professional life from those who think they are entitled. Success is blind to gender, race, ethnicity, age, upbringing, and disabilities. Success doesn't give out participation ribbons; you get no prize just because you tried. Success doesn't judge; it's there for anyone who wants it. If you are willing to do the work, I promise you, it will be worth it.

M = Mastery

"Self-mastery is a challenge for every individual. Only we can control our appetites and passions. Self-mastery cannot be bought by money or fame. It is the ultimate test of our character. It requires climbing out of the deep valleys of our lives and scaling our own Mount Everests."

—James E. Faust

Discover Your Why

SUCCESS IS NOT necessarily defined by fame or wealth. Only you can define what success means to you. The late, great poet laureate Maya Angelou said, "Success is liking yourself, liking what you do, and liking how you do it." To me, success is the ability to live your dream! To live your dream, you must understand your purpose in life. We can't master something we have not identified. If you don't know what your target is, I guarantee you will hit it 100% of the time.

A few months ago, I went to the podiatrist to get my foot examined. The doctor walked in and we quickly developed a rapport. I watched him as he prepared his tools to biopsy my foot. He was smart, well-dressed, educated and had a thriving business. As I sat on the examining table, I was thinking *this guy is living his dream.*

I asked if he liked what he did for a profession. His reply was short, honest, and blunt. He said, "No, not really, but it pays the bills." I must admit, his answer surprised me. According to society and how we normally define success, he met the criteria. He had made it through years of higher education, he was a doctor, had a growing business, made excellent money, and was in the business of helping people. We can all agree that he had accomplished many things, but he was not successful because, in his mind, he was not living his purpose.

Most people, like my podiatrist, are just going to a JOB, which stands for *just over bored*. Many people are just going through the motions every day to pay the bills, like my podiatrist, but wish they could be pursuing their dream.

The most important question you can ever answer for yourself is *what is my purpose?* Another way to express this is *know your why*. Only 20% of people know their purpose in life. Most people think that their purpose is to go to work and make a living, but that's being driven by greed and fear—two emotions that will keep them from success. Greed, because they need the money, and fear, because if they don't have the money, they can't pay their bills. Yes, I understand you need a job but there is a difference between doing something you love for money and doing something *because* you love money. You may already be in a job that is your purpose. Congratulations!

For most people, their job is merely a vehicle to support them until they find their purpose.

When you truly know your purpose in life, you start living the life you love. Mark Twain said, "The two most important days in your life are the day you are born and the day you find out why." When you are alone, ask yourself, "What is my purpose?" And yes, talk out loud, because your brain thinks differently when it hears your voice. If you can't answer that question, then it's the start of an important journey to discover and master your purpose in life. It may take you days, months, or even years, but don't stop trying to identify your purpose. You may discover that you have more than one purpose. You may have a family, personal, and career purpose all at the same time.

It wasn't until my late thirties that I truly discovered my purpose. The reason it took me so long was because I never took the time to identify my purpose in life. No one asked, either. My purpose in life is to study large amounts of information about how people can succeed in life, simplify that information, then deliver the information in a way that will inspire others to pursue their dreams. Once I was able to identify my purpose, my life started to change.

Some questions you should ask yourself that will help you find your purpose are:

- "What do I like to do?"

- "What am I good at?"

- "What am I passionate about?"

- "What could I do all day long and not worry about receiving a paycheck, but I do it so well people would want to pay me for it?"

- "What would get me out of bed each morning without an alarm clock, excited about my day?"

- "What would I love to do so much that I would be willing to make sacrifices?"

- "If you only had one year left to live, what would you start doing tomorrow?"

Those are just a few questions to get you started on your way to finding your purpose.

What makes you come alive? The word inspire comes from the Latin *inspirare*, meaning to breathe life into. Accordingly, when you are working toward things that inspire you, it literally makes you feel more alive. When you feel alive, you are probably living your why, which is your purpose. Oprah Winfrey said, "Follow your passion. It will lead you to your purpose."

Your Why Should Make You Cry

YOUR WHY SHOULD make you cry. If it doesn't, then your purpose is not strong enough. Until your story of your why is bigger than your story of why you can't, you never will. When you go on the journey of identifying your purpose, ask yourself why at least three times. The more you drill down on the why question, the more inspired you will be to act upon your purpose or goal.

I was working with a client who wanted to lose twenty pounds. It's an admirable goal, but I knew it probably wasn't going to motivate her to get out of bed at 5 a.m. to go for a walk unless she applied the 3x why concept. I asked, "What is your goal?" She replied, "To lose twenty pounds." "Why do you want to lose twenty pounds?" She said, "Because I want to feel better about myself." I continued, "Why do you want to feel better about yourself?" She said, "Because with the extra weight I have low self-esteem, and since I have low self-esteem, I attract the wrong people into my life." I kept digging, "Why is important to you to have the right people in your life?" She broke down and said, "Right now, I'm letting the wrong people in my life and they are using me. I allow them to treat me badly. If I had higher self-esteem, I would be more confident to hang around winners instead of losers."

By drilling down on the why question, I was able to extract the real reason she wanted to lose the weight. I also hit an emotional chord with her and took her on a journey she had never expressed to herself. I promise you she started getting out of bed at 5 a.m. to walk, because her why made her cry (literally). If we had just left the goal as a number of pounds, it would not have been as motivating.

Another client I was coaching had the goal of getting his master's degree. I used the same technique as I did with my female client. I asked, "Why do you want your master's degree?" He said, "So I can get a better job." I continued, "Why do you want a better job?" He said, "To make more money." I was thinking, *drill baby, drill*. I said, "Why do you want to make more money?" He said, "Well, my parents are elderly, and I will have to support them in a few years." Bingo! Supporting his elderly parents is a why that will make him cry and be willing to overcome the obstacles to pursing his master's degree.

Think of a four-year-old being in your kitchen, and their why is chocolate-chip cookies. At four years old, your why is simple. Let's pretend you have homemade, freshly-baked, chocolate-chip cookies in your cookie jar on top of your refrigerator, and you walk out of the room. Will the four-year-old find a way to get the cookies? You bet they will! They will climb on the kitchen swivel chair, risking injury, and then swing on the cupboard handle if they have to. They will take huge risks to get the cookies, because they are focused on their why. It's no different if you are four or eighty-four. If the why is strong enough, you will achieve your goals.

Master Your Mind

GET YOUR MIND right and you will get your life right. You must master how you think and get into a positive mindset. There was a book written by Dr. Norman Vincent Peale called *The Power of Positive Thinking*, first published in 1952. The book stayed on the New York Times bestseller list for 186 consecutive weeks. According to the publisher, Simon and Schuster, the book has sold around five million copies. Since then, the topic of positive thinking has been studied by neuroscientists who, unsurprisingly, found that having a positive mindset has an enormous impact on your success.

You become what you think you are, and all your actions proceed from your thoughts. What you think creates a perception that will turn into reality. *What you think about is what you bring about.* Let's consider people who come to work on a Monday morning and say, "Geez, this is going to be a long week; today is only Monday." Guess what kind of week they are going to have? Yes, you know the answer. They are going to have a *long* week. Your brain goes into overdrive to support whatever thoughts you have. It will formulate sentences and actions to help support what you're thinking, turning them into reality. So, if you think your day is going to be bad or long—or you doubt you can do something—then your brain starts to work in ways to support what you're thinking coming true. The old saying, "garbage in, garbage out," isn't true, where our thoughts are concerned. Garbage, once in, *stays* in; it rarely ever goes out without quite a bit of effort.

Your thoughts form your character: how you operate in the world, the decisions you make, how far you travel mentally, physically, and spiritually. With every thought, your brain releases chemicals. Being focused on negative thoughts effectively saps the brain of its positive force, slows it down, and can go as far as dimming your brain's ability to function, maybe even creating depression. On the flip side, thinking positive, happy, hopeful, optimistic, joyful thoughts decreases cortisol and produces serotonin, which creates a sense of well-being. This helps your brain function at peak capacity.

Each day you will encounter changes, challenges, negative people, the unexpected, and your own story. Just because you are a positive thinker doesn't make those things go away. But when you are a positive thinker, it allows you to deal with those events more effectively.

In fact, science has proven many benefits to positive thinking. Those who truly are positive thinkers can handle more stress, set higher goals, achieve more, have less health issues, are more liked, can handle a bigger workload, are focused, motivated, better listeners, optimistic, and experience deeper meaningful relationships. The opposite is true as well. People who truly don't understand the concept of positive thinking and mastering their mind will have increased stress, more health issues, struggle in their personal relationships, and find it difficult to achieve success.

If you think you can, you can; if you think you can't, well, you're right. Mastering your mindset is the starting point if you want to *Hit Your Mark*. You become what you talk about all day long. If you tell yourself sad, negative, and depressing things, it won't be long before you become depressed. If you tell yourself positive, motivational, and happy things, your life will move in a positive direction.

Optimism vs. Pessimism

POSITIVE THINKERS ARE optimistic in life. Negative thinkers are pessimistic. Optimism comes from the Latin word *optimus*, meaning best, which describes how an optimistic person is always looking for the best in any situation and expecting good things to happen. When it comes to something difficult in life and the choice is between slim and none, optimists will choose slim every time. Optimism is the tendency to believe, expect, or hope that things will turn out well. Even if something bad happens, like the loss of a job, an optimist sees the silver lining. Pessimists think the opposite way. They blame themselves for the bad things that happen in their lives and think that one mistake means more will inevitably come. Pessimists see positive events as flukes that are outside of their control: a lucky streak that probably won't happen again.

Is your glass half full or half empty? If your glass is half full, then you will attract positive events and people into your life that will help with your success. If you live your life perceiving the glass as half empty, then you probably have low expectations of your true potential. You will attract others who think like you, and together, you can have a weekend picnic in victimhood.

Whatever you allow yourself to focus on, you will attract. Your thoughts act as an incredibly strong magnet—or repellent. The more you choose to focus on positive thoughts, the stronger your magnet will be and the more it will attract the right people and opportunities to you. If you make the choice to focus on doubt and negativity, your mind will act as a barrier to success, repelling those opportunities. The power of attraction is a universal power, manifesting everywhere and in everything. It is the power that holds the universe together. It is the power that brings thoughts into manifestation.

Your mind is an antenna, seeking signals to help you in life. If you have a positive transmission, you will start noticing positive events, people, and opportunities occurring in your life. You may mistake these coincidences as just casual connections. However, the coincidences that occur in your life are divine appointments. A coincidence in life happens when you are sending out positive vibes and recognize certain opportunities to help take your life to the next level. A mentor of mine shared with me that coincidence happens when hard work meets opportunity.

I was in the process of studying the power of attraction during a business trip to Texas. I was really working on taking my positive thinking and energy to a new level. The first day of my trip, I had four positive experiences happen that I believe were a result of the positive energy I was emitting. I was eating lunch with a gentleman named Morris, whom now I'm proud to call a friend. Morris and I were discussing authors of books that we had read. The name Jack Canfield surfaced; we both enjoy his books, especially *Chicken Soup for the Soul.* As it turns out, Morris wrote a poem that Jack used in the preface of the book. I was honored to meet Morris and extremely impressed that I was eating lunch with a man who had achieved such a great honor.

When I arrived back to the hotel that afternoon, I was ordering a sandwich from the bartender. He asked what I did for a living and I told him how I help people design a better life. As I was finishing my sandwich, he asked me to give him advice for his life. I was happy to, as he was a young man who had a good attitude and was determined. The brief encounter with the bartender allowed me to practice and sharpen my message in a limited amount of time.

On the way back to my hotel room, I shared the elevator with a man who intrigued me. He was impeccably dressed and had a good demeanor. I asked him one question, and in return, he gave me two pieces of information I will cherish for a lifetime. (I call this a micro-mentoring moment. I was mentored by a gentleman I didn't even know, on a short elevator ride.) Later that night in my hotel room, I received a call from someone I had not spoken to in ten years, which led to a business opportunity.

I went to bed that night wondering how many other opportunities in life I may have missed by not always sending out a positive vibe. I also thought about my amazing day and having four spontaneous divine appointments that were put in my path all because I was focused on the right type of things. Where is your focus? Are you sending out a positive vibe to attract the right people and opportunities or are you building a mental wall, so nothing gets through? Remember, your mind is like a magnet; it will attract what you think.

Whatever you think about most is where your energy will flow and magnify in your life. Whatever you focus on the longest becomes the strongest. If you get up every morning and think about your financial problems, then your financial problems will expand and get worse. If you think all day about how you don't feel well, you will delay feeling better. On the other hand, if you get up and think positive things, you will reap the rewards.

What is your mind transmitting throughout the day? Would you agree that you could be just 5% more positive? Are you willing to put in the work to master your mind? Make no mistake, it will take hard work. Thomas Edison said, "Opportunity is missed by most people because it's dressed in overalls and looks like work." I know you will give it a try to increase your positive vibes, or you wouldn't be reading this book.

Change Your Attitude, Change Your Life

WHEN I HIT the bottom in my life, I met a gentleman who told me I didn't have a life problem, I had an attitude problem. When he told me that, I was a little offended; I thought I had a good attitude. He explained to me that sometimes good is not good enough. He wanted me to think about what he told me for a couple days, and if I was willing to try to have an open mind, he was willing to work with me.

I did some internal reflecting and realized I needed his help. I had nothing to lose, since I literally didn't have anything to lose. I knew if I wanted my life to change, I needed to master my attitude. I called him back and was at his mercy. For the next several months, I listened to every word he said and didn't doubt the process.

The first thing I learned is that everything starts with mastering a great attitude. For each level you improve your attitude, you will improve your life just as much. If your attitude is good, make it great. If your attitude is great, make it unforgettable. You always can take your attitude to the next level, no matter how good or great you think it already is.

Everything in life leads back to your attitude. According to Zig Ziglar, "Your attitude, not your aptitude, determines your altitude," meaning how successful and fulfilled you feel in your life is dependent on your attitude. Your attitude is either leading the way, or it's in the way; either connecting you or disconnecting you; either working for you or against you; either helping you or hurting you.

There are two very important concepts to remember about your attitude. The first important thing to keep in mind is that *only you can choose your attitude*. Nobody else can make the choice of what attitude you wear for the day. The second thing is that *your attitude teaches others how you want to be treated*. Those who have a great attitude send out a positive signal and others will want to help, work for, and support them. The reverse is true as well. People will shy away, ignore, or even run from people with a negative attitude.

The one thing that can change your life in an instant is mastering your attitude. If you truly want to reach the power of positive thinking, your attitude must be positive. I have never met anyone with a negative attitude who is a positive thinker. I applied this one simple concept to my life and noticed in a very short time that the more I worked on my improving my attitude, the more my life started to improve.

Unfortunately, we all know people who have a negative attitude. The frustrating thing about those with a negative attitude is that they're in denial and the last to know they have a negative attitude. I refer to this as stinkin'-thinkin'. The terms stinkin'-thinkin' is one popularized by the recovery community. It's used to describe self-destructive thought processes and self-doubt. Such thinking can cripple the human spirit. It can lead to depression and stops people from getting the most out of life.

Often people will act out in a negative way (unknowingly) when they are dealing with something they don't want to confront. It could be something they are struggling with such as finances, relationships, health, or their self-image. Negative people frequently project their negative attitude onto others, which reflects how they are feeling internally.

Imagine a driver going at or just below the speed limit in the fast lane, holding up other cars and not moving to a slower lane. The driver is either clueless that they are holding up traffic or has made the decision that they are going fast enough, and it's up to the other cars to deal with their driving. People who have a negative attitude are similar. They are either unaware that their attitude is in the gutter, or they don't care and expect everyone around them to deal with it.

I was mentoring a woman a few years ago who was the top producer in her office. She was very smart, articulate, driven, organized, and a good critical thinker. She epitomized everything a boss could want from an employee. The problem was, she had been passed over for promotion three years in a row. It didn't take me long after working with her to figure out why such a talented employee was not being selected. It was her attitude. Her attitude was horrible, to put it mildly. She was a very negative person and I must admit, after spending only a few minutes with her, I was completely drained.

The sad part of the story is that I knew what was wrong, but I couldn't help her because she was in denial. She wasn't being honest with herself, and she became very defensive when I brought up the subject. She eventually moved on to another job, and guess what? She didn't like the job because she wasn't advancing. Do you see the issue? It was never the job or the organization; it was her attitude. This is what you call destination disease. People think they will be happier when they get a new job, house, or spouse—but they are still stuck with themselves. Their negative attitude follows them wherever they go. One of the unfortunate things I have learned by working with many people is that some people won't participate in their own rescue. If they are not willing to improve their attitude, then all other advice will go unheard.

To master your attitude takes some soul searching and asking yourself where your attitude ranks daily. Could it be better? You must look in the mirror and mentally expose yourself. You must be willing to be emotionally buck naked to realize there is room for improvement. Without being honest with yourself, chances are, you will remain complacent in life. Self-honesty is too many times underrated, but it's a critical pillar to moving ahead. While being honest with yourself takes courage, avoid being too critical of yourself to the point that it demotivates you. Self-honesty and self-discovery are about knowing, learning, and improving.

All this may seem overwhelming, but I assure you, it' isn't. You have an attitude toward everything important in your life, such as your health, wealth, career, and relationships. Your attitude toward each of those things will determine the decisions you make, which will determine your outcome.

You can look at someone who is fit and know what their attitude is toward their health. They obviously have a great attitude for being healthy, and therefore make better eating choices and exercise on a regular basis; that's why they look fit and healthy. The same is true for your relationships. If your attitude is great toward your relationships, you will make better choices and reap the awards of meaningful friendships. Your attitude determines your choices, which deliver your outcomes. If you want better outcomes, make better choices; to make better choices, master having a great attitude.

The one common denominator I have observed that separates those who have reached success, lived their dreams, and are fulfilled in life from those always wishing for success was their attitude. Are you a pretender or a contender? Contenders work daily on their attitude and have acute awareness when it needs to improve. Pretenders think their attitude is good enough.

Keep the Power

HAVING A POSITIVE attitude is not about trying to impress other people. You are making the choice to do it for yourself, because you know it's a key pillar to *Hit Your Mark*. You have decided that good is not good enough, and your attitude will now range from great to exceptional.

However, watch out! If you truly decide to have a consistent, exceptional attitude, you will not fit in with the conformers anymore. Some people will quietly admire you; some will be confused, often avoiding you; some will watch and study your change; some will be upset, if not downright angry; and some will be jealous, developing such a sense of envy at your happiness that they want to bring you down to their level and make you conform.

Imagine if you made the choice to go into your place of work and demonstrate a consistent, superb attitude. What would the others around you want to do to you? They would want to reach in their bag, pull out an arrow, and shoot you in the back. They will want to bring you down to their level, forcing you to join them in their average life.

For some reason, many people will develop a jealous attitude and feel envy toward people who have a consistently great attitude. Sometimes, they are driven by their jealous attitude in such a way that they voice passive-aggressive comments, hurling them like spears. Ignore those people who are constantly talking about you behind your back, because they are right where they belong: *behind you.* If people are jealous of you, it means you are worth something.

Sometimes, we unknowingly give toxic individuals influence over our thoughts, behaviors, and feelings and let them ruin our day. People with negative attitudes can monopolize your time, even when they're not with you. It's important to always be aware of your attitude and regain your personal power. Negative people should get the least of our time and energy, yet we often give them the most attention.

You must guard your attitude like a momma bear guards her cubs. Just because you have a great attitude most of the time doesn't mean your attitude won't slip now and then. I once was waiting for a shuttle bus at a large business complex. As I walked by a group of people, a young woman joking with her coworkers said, "Watch what you say; here comes Mr. Positive Attitude." They all turned and giggled at me. I stopped, went over and just gave her a confused look. She knew she had struck a chord inside me.

She then asked, "Don't you ever have bad days?" I explained to her and the group that just because I strive for a great attitude and am a positive thinker doesn't mean I don't have bad days, or that I don't get cranky, argue, get frustrated, or get irate. I am human. But when I catch my attitude slipping, I immediately recognize what is happening and try to make the change. If I don't, it will not benefit me or others around me. I do not allow negative people to determine how I think, feel, and behave. Striving for an excellent attitude every day allows me the power to use my time and energy for becoming my best self.

The shuttle bus came, the group got on the bus one by one, and there was silence. As the bus drove away, the woman who made the comment looked out the window and flashed me a smile, letting me know she understood my message. I'm willing to bet she made the choice to have a better attitude for the rest of the day, as well as those who were with her. Your attitude has a ripple effect. If you touch one person in a positive light with your attitude, it may improve their attitude, which will affect others the rest of the day.

Smiling Is Contagious

TO IMPROVE YOUR attitude immediately, just smile. I know, it almost sounds too simple. You may be thinking *that's common sense, right?* What I have learned about common sense is that common sense is not so common. If you know something but aren't doing it, then you don't *know* it. There is more to a smile than meets the eye. Therefore, it's the fastest way to start feeling better about life.

We have neurons in our brain with a synchronizing feature, which keeps us in sync with those we are speaking to. If they smile, we smile! Those of you who are parents and grandparents enjoy spending time with your children or grandchildren in part because, on average, a child will smile 400 times per day. When they smile, you smile. On average, adults smile as little as 20 times per day, and sometimes, as little as five times per day. Do you see the problem?

We have become a stressed-out society. To improve your attitude, you might have to loosen up a little bit. Enjoy this journey called life. I guarantee you that you won't look back on life ten years from now and say, "Man, if I was just a little more tense, I would have been more successful," or "If I was just a little more demanding, I would have had more meaningful relationships in my life."

I once was coaching a gentleman who told me that he has a great attitude, but he wasn't into the whole "smiling thing." When he told me that, I laughed. I'm still trying to wrap my mind around his statement. I have never met anyone with a great attitude who didn't like to smile.

Smiling not only improves your attitude, it also improves your overall health. A study suggests that holding a smile on one's face during periods of stress may help the heart. The study, published in *Psychological Science*, lends support to the adage "grin and bear it," suggesting it may also make us feel better.

The study is the work of psychological scientists Tara Kraft and Sarah Pressman of the University of Kansas. They looked at how different types of smiling, and people being aware of smiling, affected their ability to recover from stressful episodes. They found smiling not only signals happiness to others, but it could also be a way to help cope with life's stressors.

We start to smile long before we are even born. Researchers from

Durham University discovered fetuses try out facial expressions such as grimacing, furrowing their brows, and wrinkling their nose long before they are born. If you think about it, babies who are born blind know how to smile without ever seeing a smile to mimic. Smiling is something we are born with, not something that is learned. It puzzles me that we are born with the beautiful gift called a smile, and then most of our lives, especially as we grow older, we find ways not to use that gift.

When you smile, endorphins are released; chemicals that can improve your attitude, among other things. Smiling also lowers blood pressure. The saying "fake it 'til you make it," applies here. Even if you are not feeling well, or are feeling stressed, force a smile and your body will start responding in a better way.

Contrary to what we may have been led to believe, it takes more muscles to smile than to frown. According to a study done by Dr. David Song of the University of Chicago Medical Center, the average frown requires eleven muscles, while an average smile requires twelve. But there is a catch; even though smiling uses more muscles, it is believed smiling takes less effort than frowning. This is because people tend to smile more, which means the relevant muscles are in better shape. When muscles are in better shape, they require less energy (effort) when used.

Remember, everything in your life stems from your attitude, and you can improve your attitude right now just by smiling. Even if you are by yourself, and there is no one to see, smile anyway. *Do it for you.* Use the power of manifestation. When you act a certain way, your mind and body will follow. When I get cut off in traffic or stressed, the first thing I do is smile. I know that if I do it often enough, my thoughts change and my actions follow. I create my happiness through smiling. When you smile, you will not only feel better, you will also look better.

Knowledge

IN THIS ECONOMY, people get paid based on their knowledge, skills, and abilities. What do you know? What skills do you have that place you at the top of your field? What abilities do you have to help yourself or others succeed? Mastering knowledge, skills, or ability is critical to moving your life to the next level. Being average is over. Average is poverty; nobody remembers second place. People want to pay masters, not jacks of all trades. Many people try to spread themselves thin over many subject areas and end up becoming master of nothing. It's good to have back-up plans and be diverse, but you must be clear on your mastery. You know you have reached mastery in your area of expertise when you do something and people say, "Wow; do that again."

I once owned a small entertainment business. At first, it focused on providing DJ services at weddings. As a hobby, I like to perform magic, so I added that to the list of services. A month later I added balloon delivery and face painting. It seemed like I was adding a new service every month. You can predict the rest of this story. The business never succeeded, and I moved on to other adventures at a huge financial loss. I failed because I tried being the jack of all trades, instead of really mastering one line of business before adding to my menu.

The average person reads one book per year. According to leading author and speaker, Brian Tracey, if you read 50–60 books in one subject area, you will have the equivalent of a PhD in that topic. Keep in mind that drive time is learning time, as well. What are you listening to in your car? The average person spends 101 minutes in their car every day. If you were to listen to an audio book, you could finish one book every two or three days.

To have mastery of your expertise, you may have to attend a conference to meet people in your industry, getting new ideas and seeing what others are doing. Watch free TED videos. Take a class online, through a massive open online course (MOOC). Ask to follow someone around (shadow them) in a field you may be interested in pursuing.

A young man once approached Socrates and asked the famous philosopher how he could acquire wisdom and knowledge.

"Follow me," Socrates said in response, as he led the young man down to the sea. The young man followed as Socrates began wading through the water, first at ankle depth, then knee, then waist, and finally to shoulder height.

Then, rather abruptly, Socrates grabbed the young man and dunked him under the water. The young man struggled desperately and just before he blacked out, Socrates pulled him up.

Infuriated, the young man screamed, "What are you doing?! Trying to kill me?!"

Calmly, Socrates responded, "Absolutely not. If that was my intention, I would not have pulled you up."

"Then why did you just do that?" the young man gasped.

"When you want wisdom and insight as badly as you desired that breath of air, then you shall have it."

I study almost every night. Why? I have a hunger for being in the top of the training and speaking industry. Formal education will get you a job, but self-education will make you a fortune. Don't ever think you have arrived; that will just make you ignorant and arrogant. Don't ever think you are at the point in life that you can stop learning. Once you stop learning, you stop leading; once you stop leading, you start losing. The power of learning is that once the mind has been expanded with an idea, concept, or experience, it can never be satisfied with going back to where it was.

You must be obsessed with the idea of being a master in your area of interest. Grant Cardone, the inventor of the 10X Rule said, "Be obsessed or be average." Whatever it takes, you must be committed to be the best version of yourself in mastering your topic. People who are committed to mastery want to be in the top 10% of their field because they know the bottom is overcrowded. One of my favorite quotes is by J.G. Holland: "God gives every bird its food, but he does not throw it into the nest." We are surrounded by knowledge in an information age when you can obtain most of what you need to know for free—but it's up to you to make the time, put in the effort, and have a thirst for knowledge. When you are obsessed with being a master in your field, you will become unstoppable. You should always be working harder on yourself than at your job, because when you become great at who you are, you will become awesome at what you do.

Gratitude

BEING GRATEFUL IS an extension of being thankful. If you think you are already grateful, push yourself to be more grateful and take it to the level of mastery. Make it a pillar in your life to live with an attitude of gratitude. When something positive happens in life, it's easy to be grateful. But having an attitude of gratitude is not an event; it's a constant state of mind, being appreciative even during the challenging times. As I look back in my life, I'm grateful for my struggles; they helped me stumble across my strengths.

An attitude of gratitude is just not being appreciative of the big stuff, it's also about recognizing all the small stuff that we see, hear, taste, touch, and experience every day. Be grateful for everything you have. You have no idea how many people would love to have what you've got.

The first step to increasing your level of gratitude is to start becoming more aware in life. You are reading this book, which means you're awake, alive, and literate, so you can be grateful for waking up this morning and knowing how to read. God's gift to you is life and how you live your life is your gift back to God. William Ward said, "Feeling gratitude and not expressing it is like wrapping a present and not giving it." Being more grateful may seem easy, but it's difficult because we live in a fast-paced world. We need to slow down to appreciate the small things—or, as the old saying goes, take time to smell the roses.

Besides paying attention to the small things that make life awesome, the second most important thing about being grateful is to journal your gratitude. This is key to cultivating a better attitude of gratitude. At the minimum, you should spend five minutes every day to write down three things that you are grateful for. I want you to write down a fourth thing, as well: what you are grateful for about yourself. Be specific, too. If you write, *I'm thankful for food*, write why you are thankful for food. If you are grateful for a coworker, write something specific about why you are grateful for your coworker. Some people will journal throughout the day to document the things they are grateful for.

Journaling for a few minutes every day will make you happier. You must stick with it for at least six months before you start seeing the rewards. There is always something to be grateful for in life.

You can even be thankful for all the difficult people in your life, and what you learn from them. *They are showing you exactly who you do not want to be.*

I'll admit, I didn't buy into journaling because to me it seemed silly. I was grateful in life, so I didn't understand why I needed to write about it. I didn't understand the power of neuroplasticity. Neuroplasticity is when you rewire your brain through specific actions. This is how stroke victims can recover from side effects caused by the stroke. When you journal your gratefulness every day, you are rewiring your brain to a level not experienced by many people. It will give you a sense of calmness and serenity.

Gratitude is an emotion that can be developed and strengthened, just like any other muscle in your body. There is a direct link between how grateful you are and how happy you feel. Gratitude affects your emotions, social life, health, career, and personality.

Journaling just a few minutes every day can increase your long-term well being by more than 10%. That's the same impact as doubling your income. Gratitude helps your career through improved decision making, networking, productivity, career management, and the ability to achieve your goals.

People with gratitude exercise more, get more sleep, have less health issues, experience more energy, and live longer. Participants in studies related to this had lower blood pressure and reduced symptoms of depression by 35%.

Gratitude affects our personality by causing us to be less materialistic, less self-centered, more optimistic, more spiritual—and increases self-esteem. It affects our emotional needs by helping us feel better, more relaxed, more resilient, and less envious, aa well as allowing us to have happier memories.

How you do anything is how you will do everything. When I started journaling, I didn't cut any corners; I was true to myself and spent quality time reflecting each day on my gratitude. It helped me realize that not every day will be a good day, but there is good in every day.

I was working with a gentleman who was complaining about his job. I had him take out a piece of paper and write a letter with no intention of sending it: using it only as an exercise. I told him to imagine that starting tomorrow, he had no job. I asked him to write a letter to his office detailing what he would miss about his job, and why. As you can imagine, he wrote: *I miss my paycheck because it allowed me to support my family. I miss the friendship of coworkers. I miss the health benefits* (because it helped cover the cost of his care for high blood pressure). By the time he finished the letter, he realized just how grateful he was toward his job. He had been caught up in the day-to-day stresses of his job and was not taking time to be grateful of the life his job was providing. Gratitude turns what we have into being enough.

Peyton Manning was the quarterback for the Denver Broncos when they won the Super Bowl in 2016. He is one of the best to ever play his position. That Super Bowl was the last game of his career. Imagine the feeling of playing your last game and winning the biggest prize in US sports. A reporter met Manning on the field for a post-game interview, surrounded by dozens of cameras and microphones. The reporter asked, "What's it like winning the Super Bowl?" Manning used the phrase "I'm grateful" three times during the one-minute interview. It shouldn't be a surprise that one of the greatest quarterbacks and athletes understands the meaning of being grateful. Be grateful every day to be alive, to be you, because you are perfect—and with gratitude, you'll attract all you ever wanted. Walt Disney said, "The more you are in a state of gratitude, the more you will attract things to be grateful for."

Forgiveness

THE GREEK WORD for forgive is *aphiemi*, meaning to let go, among other things. Learning to master forgiveness is one of the most difficult acts you will go through in your life. Forgiveness is not just a spiritual concept. It is a psychological process, as well. We must learn to forgive ourselves as well as those who have hurt and betrayed us. Forgiving does not mean forgetting, it's remembering without anger. It also doesn't mean you should give someone a second chance. Forgiveness is the journey you take to forego grief.

When people hurt you, betray you, or cross your lines of trust, it can take weeks, months, or even years to forgive them. You are not forgiving the person who hurt you to benefit them; you are doing it for yourself. If you have been wronged by someone and you have not forgiven them, they will be in your head and dominate your thoughts because whatever we think about expands. Without forgiveness, they are mentally victimizing you over and over and over. *Forgive others not because they deserve it, but because you deserve peace.*

What are you losing in life by not forgiving? Some say "nothing," but that's not true. Not forgiving is holding on to the past, which will cause increased stress, disappointment, and anger. Your body and mind are a continuum. In other words, although they are not entirely the same, a great overlap exists that unites them. Relieve your mental stress, and your body will be happier too. Nothing relieves mental stress like forgiveness. Guilt and hatred resolve nothing; they just sustain the negativity that continues to obstruct your dreams. Forgiveness, on the other hand, dissolves the stickiness binding you to an unhappy past.

I once coached a woman who had been cheated on by her husband. She never went through the process to forgive him. Therefore, he was in her mind constantly, causing depression and resentment. When you don't truly go on the journey of forgiveness, and you let the ill-spirited person stay in your head, then you will attract more of the same. What you think about, you will attract. In fact, the woman was drawn toward another man much like her ex-husband, and he too cheated on her. Since she didn't truly forgive her ex-husband, she was drawn to other men with the same attributes without even knowing it.

Imagine driving down the highway at 60 MPH and your eyes are focused on the small rearview mirror looking out the back window. What do you think would happen if you kept driving like that? You guessed it; you would crash, because you can't drive forward very far while looking backwards. That is what not forgiving looks like. When you learn to forgive, you take your eyes off the little mirror and look forward, out the large windshield. Only then can you see the beautiful mountains ahead of you.

You should forgive everyone you feel requires your forgiveness, whether they are dead or alive. You know you need to forgive someone if you feel or think you might have some anger, hurt, and/or resentment toward them. The first person who comes to mind as you are reading this is obviously a good place to start. Once you forgive people in your mind, the energy is immediately released to bring you your freedom. You do not need to contact the other person to let them know you have invoked the gift of forgiveness for it to work. Forgiveness is something you do *for yourself.*

Give people who have hurt, disappointed, humiliated, or angered you the benefit of the doubt. If they knew better, they would have done better. Some people become uncentered within themselves and operate out of low self-consciousness. People who are hurting hurt other people. It isn't an excuse for their behavior, but it will enhance your character if you can be the bigger person. Bestselling author Dr. Wayne W. Dyer has shared, "When given the choice between being right or being kind, choose kind."

Remember that the other person you must forgive is yourself. You will have many regrets in your life. The more aggressively you pursue success and happiness, the more mistakes you will make. You must forgive yourself when you make those mistakes. If you don't forgive yourself, you will be too timid to decide on the next big opportunity. Most importantly, if you don't learn to forgive yourself, you will not be able to forgive others.

When I fell to the bottom of life and made many, many mistakes, it took me a long time to forgive myself. It was the elephant on my back that I couldn't get off. Learning to forgive myself took me about two years; I had to understand and accept my mistakes. Once I understood that it's OK to forgive myself, and stop keeping myself in my mental prison, my life and success changed for the better. I realized that yesterday was my old past; today, I have the opportunity to create a new past.

It's hard to forgive yourself when you make mistakes, especially the big ones, because you will be surrounded by negative reinforcement from those closest to you. They will ask questions or make statements such as: "What were you thinking?" "How could you?" "You should have known better." All these statements reinforce the negativity, and since they are people in your inner circle, they make it harder to forgive yourself. When you forgive, it allows you to move forward with what you want in life.

Sometimes, you need to separate yourself from your daily duties to forgive, allowing your mind to reflect and heal. Go for a walk, journal, check into a hotel, talk to a friend, pray… You may find you need to seek professional help. Whatever works for you, make it a goal to let it go and free that person; in return, you will free yourself.

Forgiveness is one of the most loving and positive things you can do for yourself and others. Forgiveness breaks a bond of negativity that keeps energy tied up between you and another person or persons. If we do not forgive, we build a negative wall of energy and stop the good from coming into our lives. It is this negative energy, between you and the other person(s) you are not ready to forgive, that creates a bond between you—keeping you tied to them.

Forgiveness leads to healing, understanding, and redemption. Forgiveness leads to faith. To ask for forgiveness, a person must know what it is like to forgive. To forgive, one must know what it is like to be forgiven. Don't forget that this applies to you, too. If you have crossed someone else's boundaries, you must ask for forgiveness to set yourself free from the thoughts that probably keep occurring because you feel bad or guilty. The gift of forgiveness creates total freedom. Mark Twain supposedly said, "Forgiveness is the fragrance that the violet sheds on the heel that has crushed it."

A = Accountability

"Accountability separates the wishers in life from the action-takers that care enough about their future to account for their daily actions."

—John Di Lemme

Personal Accountability

PERSONAL ACCOUNTABILITY IS the belief that you are fully responsible for your own actions and consequences. It's a choice, a mindset, and an expression of integrity. A big step to *Hit Your Mark* is being 100% accountable with zero excuses. Own your life, own your choices, and be accountable. Even though I use the words responsibility and accountability interchangeably throughout the book, accountability is a stronger word with more meaning. Responsibility can be shared, which means the blame can also be shared. Accountability means the buck stops with you. Being responsible is good; it's a step in the right direction. But being accountable carries more weight.

Taking and accepting responsibility is a choice. You are either accepting responsibility or assigning responsibility. When you commit to being responsible, you are more proactive and self-motivated. Assigning responsibility leads to passivity and belief in fate or luck, or even worse: blaming others.

In the workplace, there are owners and renters. Being accountable makes you an owner. Renters go to their job and do only what they get paid to do. They will see a problem but won't act to fix it, because it's not on their list of responsibilities. They say, "I don't get paid enough to take care of that." Owners who are accountable see a problem and are willing to help.

They put the problem on their own shoulders to be part of the solution.

Taking responsibility in your life does not mean you are responsible for those things outside your control. However, you are responsible for how you react to those situations. Consider the principle, "Life acts. You react." This means that your reactions are under your control. In any life situation, you are always responsible for at least one thing: your reaction toward the situation in which you find yourself. You can have either a positive or a negative reaction. With the right reaction, you make better choices that can shape the outcome in your favor. Charles Swindoll said, "Life is 10% what happens to you and 90% how you react to it."

If you were to get a flat tire going to work, yes, you would be frustrated. If you took 100% responsibility for your reaction, you could still have a great day. You would get help to change the tire, go to work with a good attitude, complete some assignments, and be thankful that you weren't injured. Or, you could choose not to take responsibility for your reactions, bitching and moaning all day and complaining to everyone around you—which would hinder you and your coworkers in completing your work—and then you'd go home upset. Which scenario sounds better?

There are a couple of reasons why we don't take responsibility for our actions. One reason is that we all have the need to feel significant and have others think highly of us, causing some people to have an over-inflated opinion of themselves. These tendencies lead us to wear blinders and be in denial, which creates a false perception of ourselves and the inability to accept the truth about ourselves. At this point, we don't want to be wrong; when mistakes happen, our first reaction is to point fingers, not take responsibility. Whenever we point a finger, we have three fingers point back at us. The need to feel significant clouds our judgment, making it difficult to think objectively and accept outcomes for our actions.

Another reason for our inability to accept responsibility for our actions and behaviors can be a sense of insecurity. By taking responsibility, we feel we are admitting to being weak and powerless, or we're creating an opportunity to lose the respect of others. It may cause someone to feel they will lose their sense of value and importance.

However, when you fail to take responsibility, you put yourself at a clear disadvantage; you are approaching the situation from a position of weakness, where you become the victim of circumstance. Moreover, from this weakened position, there is nothing you can do to improve your situation. In other words, you are resigned to the fate of being powerless and incapable of making things better.

To take responsibility for your life and circumstances is incredibly empowering. It's a measure of your courage, self-confidence, self-worth, character, mental strength, toughness, and resilience. Taking responsibility is the one critical factor separating those who achieve in life and those who are complacent. When that moment to take responsibility comes, what you do—or don't do—is an indication of the type of person you really are.

Anchors Aweigh

I WAS SERVING in the Navy and my ship was sailing off the coast of Central America, searching for boats transporting drugs towards the United States. The crew had been out to sea for almost 90 days without seeing land. So, as you can imagine, my fellow shipmates were excited to hear we would be pulling into port the following week to get supplies and spend a few days on liberty. The port we were going to use did not have a pier big enough to support our ship, which meant we would have to anchor away from shore and take small boats from the ship to the shore.

A few days before pulling into port, and over 100 miles from any shoreline, the boatswain's mates performed maintenance on the main anchor, since it would be used to keep the ship in place when we reached our destination. The main anchor on a Navy ship is huge, weighing tens of thousands of pounds. By accident, too much anchor chain was released below the ship into the ocean, and the winch could not pull the anchor back up.

I was working in the Combat Information Center (CIC), which is the command center where the communications to other ships and back to shore takes place. It was early evening when the captain came into the CIC to report to the admiral on shore what had happened. Even though it was over 25 years ago, I can still picture it as though it happened yesterday. The captain explained the situation, and at the end he said, "I'm accountable."

This was a significant moment. The captain took accountability, even though it really wasn't his fault. He had trusted the crew to do the right thing with the anchor, and they had failed at the task. The captain was an honorable guy; he knew that it being his ship, ultimately anything that happened was his responsibility.

When the word spread of what the captain said to the admiral, the crew started holding themselves more accountable. Imagine if the captain had pointed fingers at the crew, which would have been easy to do; after all, they were the ones who screwed up. Blaming others would not have solved anything. Because of the incident, new procedures were put in place for how the crew would review and prepare for all future procedures. The captain was a man of character, so I'm confident he started the review process with himself, reflecting on what he could have done to prevent the accident. The captain took 100% accountability with zero excuses, and that created a culture of accountability throughout the ship.

Accountability to Ourselves

WE ARE ACCOUNTABLE to others and to ourselves. It's easier to be accountable to other people, because we don't want to disappoint them—and they may call us out on our actions or lack of actions. It's much more of a challenge to be accountable to ourselves, but it's the more important of the two types of accountability.

If you are not happy with some of the things in your life, stand in front of the mirror; the reflection looking back at you is accountable. This may sound harsh, but its reality. It isn't your preacher, teacher, mother, father, boss, the Red Cross, or any other person or organization responsible for the choices you have made that have led to the life you are living. Wherever you find yourself in life at some point, you made an appointment to be there.

Accountability is like a small snowball at the top of a hill: once it starts rolling, it gains momentum and size, influencing situations and outcomes with others around you. The reverse is true in a negative way about that same snowball, if you fail to be accountable.

If you are not willing to be accountable, then the snowball will gain speed and size, and no one around you will want to be accountable, either.

One of the main challenges we struggle with in life is holding ourselves accountable and keeping our own commitments. When was the last time you made a New Year's resolution but didn't follow through? How many times have you thought about calling a friend, but didn't pick up the phone? What about at work? Have you committed to doing something, then it didn't get done?

We are constantly not following through on many of the commitments we promise ourselves we will meet. When we break commitments to ourselves it may seem harmless, but all the broken commitments add up—eventually. We do not trust ourselves. It's not something we are consciously aware of most of the time, but it's stored in our subconscious mind. When self-trust erodes, we also start not trusting other people. I believe the lack of being accountable is the most significant reason people don't move forward in their lives. By not being accountable and not trusting ourselves, we have become a society lacking trust for each other. AP-GfK conducted a poll and found one-third of Americans say most people can't be trusted.

Therefore, we have gated communities and contracts written by lawyers that are hundreds of pages long. This affects the business environment by fostering leaders who are micromanagers. Micromanagers usually have not taken accountability for something (or many things) in their own lives. A lack of self-accountability causes a lack of self-esteem and low self-confidence, which leads them to not trust their employees. How can they, when they don't trust themselves?

You can't achieve the next step in your life without having some level of confidence and self-trust. That will only happen through creating good habits and being accountable for everything in your life, including your reactions to those events that are outside of your control. Bob Proctor said, "Accountability is the glue that ties commitment to the result."

Without personal accountability, you will never grow or improve yourself. You can tell a person's character by the way they treat insignificant people and by their level of accountability. You may have many great attributes, but they will go unrecognized without personal accountability.

Being accountable sometimes requires us to do things that are unpleasant, uncomfortable, or even downright frightening. But the benefits of being accountable far outweigh the short-lived advantages of refusing to do so. No one makes his or her life better by avoiding accountability. Assuming accountability or responsibility is also about our ability to respond to circumstances, and to choose the attitudes, actions, and reactions that shape the outcome. It is a concept of power that puts us in the driver's seat. Accountable people not only depend on themselves, they also show others that they can be depended on, which allows them to have the highest form of integrity. This breeds trust, and trust is a key that opens many doors.

> "This is a story of four people named Everybody, Somebody, Anybody, and Nobody. There was an important job to be done and Everybody was asked to do it. Everybody was sure Somebody would do it. Anybody could have done it, but Nobody did it. Somebody got angry about that, because it was Everybody's job. Everybody thought Anybody could do it, but Nobody realized that Everybody wouldn't do it. It ended that Everybody blamed Somebody when Nobody did what Anybody could have done."
>
> —Anonymous

Play Ball

LET'S LOOK AT an example of personal accountability that won the hearts and minds of millions due to one person's integrity. Over 140 years of Major League Baseball history, there have been only 23 official perfect games. A perfect game is defined by Major League Baseball as a game in which a pitcher (or combination of pitchers) pitches a victory that lasts a minimum of nine innings, and in which no opposing player reaches base. Thus, the pitcher (or pitchers) cannot allow any hits, walks, hit batsmen, or any opposing player to reach base safely for any other reason: in short, 27 players up (three per inning over nine innings), 27 down.

On June 2, 2010, at Comerica Park in Detroit, Michigan, Detroit Tigers pitcher Armando Galarraga nearly became the 21st pitcher in Major League history to throw a perfect game. Facing the Cleveland Indians, Galarraga retired the first 26 batters. Jason Donald of the Detroit Tigers hit a soft ground ball in the infield and ran toward first base. He was clearly out, but the umpire Jim Joyce incorrectly ruled that Jason Donald reached first base safely. Pitcher Armando Glarraga's perfect game came to an end; his chance to become the 21st pitcher to throw a perfect game was ruined by Jim Joyce's blown call. This was huge, because this would have also marked the first perfect game in the Tigers' 110-year history. The 83 pitches thrown before the blown call would have been the fewest pitches in a perfect game since 1908.

After the game, umpire Jim Joyce saw the replay in the clubhouse and knew he had blown an important call. He immediately asked to see pitcher Armando Galarraga and gave him a tearful apology. Jim Joyce took accountability for his call and did the right thing. Taking accountability means doing the right thing over doing things that are easy.

Galarraga was forgiving and understanding of the mistake. In fact, Galarraga and Joyce made a very rare joint appearance at the post-game news conference. Galarraga was not responsible for what had happened to him, but being a true professional, he knew he was 100% accountable for his reaction. Galarraga told reporters after the game, "Nobody's perfect." Both people involved took accountability for their actions. Joyce took accountability for the blown call, and Galarraga took responsibility by controlling his reaction to the situation, which controlled the outcome.

Galarraga obviously couldn't change the outcome of the game with his reaction, but because he didn't overreact, kept his attitude in check, and accepted the apology, he showed character and integrity that earned him respect from around the world. Joyce gained support and praise from players and coaches around the league for taking accountability for the blown call.

Less than two weeks after the controversial game, *ESPN The Magazine* released an anonymous poll of 100 current MLB players that named Joyce as the best umpire in Major League Baseball. This is a great story of how one person took accountability for a mistake they made, and the person on the receiving end took accountability for their reaction, which created a positive outcome.

Armando Galarraga and Jim Joyce, along with Daniel Paisner, released a book titled *Nobody's Perfect*, chronicling their experiences during and after the game. Due to the book release, the two are now business partners. Imagine if one of them hadn't taken accountability. If Joyce tried to make excuses about the blown call, he would have lost respect in the baseball community; instead, he gained respect by admitting he had made a mistake. What if Galarraga remained bitter and complained, blaming Joyce for not achieving a perfect game? He would have never had the opportunity to write a

book with Joyce or become his business partner.

Values

TO BE ACCOUNTABLE TO ourselves and other people, we must identify our values. Knowing your values is key to determining what you do with your time and how you evaluate the time that you spend. At the deepest level of your programming, your core values drive you to spend your time in ways that support what is most important to you. Until you know what your values are, this is happening at the subconscious level.

Your top five values are the most influential on how you live your life. While others exist and are important, they do not have as much influence on your behaviors, nor can they help you prioritize your time. By becoming consciously aware of your values, you can use them to make more informed decisions and set better, clearer goals. What are three to five words or short phrases that you would tell other people to define your values? It's nearly impossible to be accountable to yourself, or have others be accountable to you, without identifying and sharing your values.

Early in my career, I was interviewing for a prestigious job. I made it through the initial process to be considered one of four potential candidates. The last phase was to be interviewed by a board of three people. I was cruising along in the board interview thinking *I'm doing well; I'm sure I will get the job.* And then the dreaded last question came, the one that caught me flat- footed. Someone on the panel asked, "Mr. Jarema, please tell us your top three values, what they mean to you, and what they will mean to the people you will be leading." Wow! I didn't have a quick answer, and the panel knew I'd never taken the time to think about it before. Because I could not articulate my answer with any confidence at all, I didn't get the job. To this day, it's still the best interview question I have ever been asked.

I was once coaching a senior executive, and I asked him what his values were. Like many people, one of his top five values was family. I knew the problem right away. One of his priority values was family, but he was working until early evening every night. His work habits and values were in direct conflict with each other.

If you don't know your values, how are you able to make critical decisions? When you know your values, they help you define who you are and what you stand for. It won't make tough decisions easier, but it will make you feel better that you are making a critical decision based on your values. Your values are the things that you believe are important in the way you live and work. They (should) determine your priorities, and deep down, they're probably the measures you use to tell if your life is turning out the way you want it to.

In life, you have people and possessions that you value, and you have values: the pillars of your character that define who you are and what you believe. While you grow as an adult and pursue your true north, any number of forces have the potential to pull you off course. Pressure can cause people to forget what they believe. However, if you can draw on your values when times get tough, you will have the courage and discipline to stay on course. You must decide *before* it's time to decide. That way, when it's time, you already have your decision.

Values are who you are in your own deepest nature, not who you *think* you should be to fit in. When the way you think, speak, and behave match your values, life feels very good; you feel whole, and content in your power. But when these don't align with your personal values, things feel...*wrong*. Life feels uneasy. You feel out of touch, discontented, restless, unhappy.

"'Cheshire Cat,' asked Alice. 'Would you tell me please, which way I ought to go from here?' 'That depends a good deal on where you want to go,' said the Cat. 'I don't much care where,' said Alice. 'Then it doesn't matter where you go,' said the Cat."

—Lewis Carrol

Mastermind Groups

THE CONCEPT OF the "master mind alliance" was introduced by Napoleon Hill in his book from the 1920s, *The Law of Success*, and expanded upon in his 1930s book, *Think and Grow Rich*. While Napoleon Hill called it a master mind alliance, it's been shortened and modernized to "mastermind group." Mastermind groups have been around since the beginning of time.

Henry Ford, Thomas Edison, Alexander Graham Bell, Theodore Roosevelt, John D. Rockefeller, and Charles Schwab all belonged to a mastermind group. Benjamin Franklin belonged to such a group, which he called the Junto Club, also known as the Leather Apron Club.

Napoleon Hill encouraged people to gather together in a structured, repeatable environment for the success of all. Hill wrote about the mastermind group principle as: "The coordination of knowledge and effort of two or more people, who work toward a definite purpose, in the spirit of harmony," and "No two minds ever come together without thereby creating a third, invisible intangible force, which may be likened to a third mind."

Mastermind groups are often called accountability groups. The agenda is set by the group, and each person's participation and commitment are key. The group can discuss what the topics will be, or you can use the chapters from a specific book or author. Meetings should last no less than one hour and should not exceed 90 minutes. This timing has been tested and proven over many years and in many situations. It can become very easy to feel like "they really wanted to talk longer," but this can also leave others who have made the same time commitment feel as if their time is not important.

Your mastermind partners give you feedback, help you brainstorm new possibilities, and set up accountability structures that keep you focused and on track. You create a community of supportive people who challenge each other to new heights.

The construct of a mastermind group can be all from the same profession or from various professions. I have hosted many leadership mastermind groups with leaders who represented different companies. The one thing they all had in common was challenging themselves to become better leaders.

I am a member of two mastermind groups. One group consists of eight members located throughout the world who are professional speakers and instructors. We meet every Sunday morning on Skype. The leader conducts the call from India. We set a goal each week, then gather for an hour to discuss our assignments and provide support to each other.

My mastermind group is invaluable, since they know my profession. They know the struggles I have because they are in the same business. They understand what is going on behind the scenes and give me support despite any challenges. They also provide me with different perspectives and resources, in addition to holding me accountable to goals.

The other mastermind group I belong to consists of super-high achievers who are experts in their fields and have reached a level in life I am striving to acquire. Technically, I don't fit the criteria financially to be in the group. However, a mentor of mine has allowed me into the group to expand my thinking and knowledge of what is possible for myself. I'm grateful for the opportunity to rub elbows with those who are making an impact in the world.

Mastermind groups are win-win, since everyone in the group will have different strengths, weaknesses, and talents. You will have a chance to help others, and they will help you. Some of the best business ideas have come about because of brainstorming sessions in a mastermind group. The support you receive will continue beyond just the brainstorming stage. Everyone will become invested in each other's success!

Your Vibe Is Your Tribe

WHO IS PART of your tribe? Taking accountability for whom you hang out with is up to you. You must surround yourself with highly collaborative, achievement-driven, supportive people who will stretch and challenge you. Surround yourself with people you can learn from, those who will help you grow, to become a better version of yourself. You want people around you who are hungry and determined, like you.

This may be a good time for you to evaluate and upgrade your relationships. Not everyone can have a seat on your bus to success. Important decisions you will constantly make throughout your life are who do you need to get on your bus to success, and who needs to get off your bus? You may have to leave some people behind. This is a tough decision—but a critical one, if you are to achieve your dreams. Just because someone is in your life doesn't mean you have to let them into your inner circle.

You can't be everyone's friend, and not everyone will deserve your friendship. Do not fall victim to the belief that your gifts, talents, and willpower are enough to overcome whatever influences your friends or acquaintances may have on you. Negative people will pull you into their difficult mental and emotional situations. Negative people allowed into your inner circle act as a cancer, eating at you as if they were a slowly spreading disease; if not monitored and dealt with, they will eventually consume you. Some people are so negative they develop when they walk into a dark room. (*Ba-dum tss!*) There are not enough tissues for their issues.

Successful people are careful to attract those who are like-minded and repel those whom they do not wish to be like. Make friends with people who share the same energy and zest for life that you do. You want your inner circle to always bring you up, never down. Get to know individuals who are smarter than you, and more experienced. Work with people who will challenge your opinions in an effective and intellectual way. You want to be encouraged and focused, not crestfallen and distracted by someone else's lack of productivity.

Lazy, unproductive, and negative friends and/or coworkers are nothing but dead weight and should be treated as such. They will pull you down and fill your head with doubt. Why on Earth would you want to hang out with someone who has no interest in making you a better person? Never take advice from people more miserable than you. Keep your distance from people with ridiculous problems, because before you know it, their issues can become yours. Then you're back at square one.

It can be a lonely place, and at times, you may feel that you are on an island with your thinking. What may surprise you is that you are not alone; many successful people have very small inner circles. It isn't about the quantity of people, it's about *quality*. Surround yourself with people who will inspire you, transform you, and push you to meet your goals and live your dreams.

Remember the letters OQP, which stands for *only quality people*. There are those people we know who bring energy into our lives, and those we hang out with that will suck all the passion out of our lives. Some people, if you never saw them again, it would still be too soon. If you hang out with ducks, you will quack; if you hang out with eagles, you will soar.

Dr. Dennis Kimbro said, "If you are the smartest one in your group, you've got to get a new group." Are you hanging out with people you can learn from? Will they stretch you beyond what you think is possible? Or are you hanging around with a group of people in which you are always at the top? If you make $20K per year and want to make $100K per year, you must hang out with people who make $100K per year. There was an MIT study that showed you will make within two to three thousand dollars of the people you hang out with the most.

Surround yourself with a community of achievers. It's the law of attraction; like-minded people hang out together. You will notice in life that high achievers don't hang out with small-minded people, because they know that small-minded people will not understand their big dreams.

Assemble Your Team

WHOM DO YOU have enrolled in your vision? Early in my career, I didn't understand the power of assembling a team of mentors and coaches to help me. I was too stubborn or embarrassed to ask for help. I thought I could just figure out my way to the top. It wasn't until I started to hit my mark in life that I realized the better way: *the bigger your dream, the bigger your team.*

I was watching a special on TV about a man who tried several times to climb Mt. Everest but didn't make it to the top. He came to the self-realization that he did not have the right people helping him. He finally assembled a team of experts, including a high-altitude breathing expert, a nutritionist, an expert in ice climbing, someone who was an expert in surviving in the cold, and a few others who could help. On his next attempt, he made it to the top of the mountain.

If you want to walk up a little hill, you can do that by yourself in your work clothes. But if you want to climb Mt. Everest, you would never attempt that by yourself in your normal clothing. You would need to assemble and rely on a team of people to help you achieve your goal. A popular (supposedly) African Proverb states, "If you want to go fast, go alone. If you want to far, go together."

When you look at all successful companies, they have a board of directors. The board meets monthly or quarterly with the chief executive officer (CEO) and other key stakeholders of the company. Think for a moment about why a smart CEO of a company would need likeminded businesspeople to meet with him or her.

Some of the reasons you may have thought of are: to review the company direction, provide advice to the leaders, or recognize the blind spots of the CEO. These are all good reasons why every company has a board of directors. Simplified, it's the same reason schools and communities have boards of directors: A *collection* of minds is much better than one mind.

To pursue your dreams, you will need to assemble your board of directors, otherwise called your dream team. You are the CEO of your own dreams. Nobody is going to care more about your career, life, and dreams than you. The good news is that there are plenty of people willing to help, but it's up to you to seek them out and ask for their help. When we go for our dreams, we need to make sure we put the right people on our board of directors.

There will be times when we fall down and can't get back up. We all fall. If you haven't fallen yet, it's only a matter of time. On occasion, you may fall and not be able to get back up mentally. If you don't fall, there will be times you will run into a brick wall and not know how to break through it. Having accountability partners can help, in those times we can't pick ourselves up or break through to the other side.

Not long ago, I ran into a mental wall and was having trouble thinking of ways to break through. I felt stuck, like I wasn't moving forward. I went to a conference and met someone I immediately added to my circle of influence. Spending time with him opened my eyes to new ideas and new ways I could get to the next level. He saw capabilities and things in me that I did not recognize. Sometimes you have to believe in others' belief in you, until your own belief kicks in.

I have assembled a team of advisors who help me continue to improve myself and work toward my goals. A good friend of mine, whom I respect and call a mentor, meets with me once a month at

Bob Evans for breakfast at 6 a.m., before his day starts. It works out perfectly; because we do not have any work distractions, we are able to cover a lot of ground in a short period of time.

Every few months you should review who is on your team to determine if you need to rotate members out or seek new ones. Maybe you will only need someone's help for a short period of time, to learn a new skill or make a connection. Not everyone on your team needs to be a long-term member.

When you ask someone to be a member of your advisory board or dream team, be sensitive to wasting their time. People are extremely busy, especially those in senior positions or those who are very successful. They will probably be willing to help—however, they will be more willing to help you if they know you won't waste their time. Before meeting with any of your mentors, you owe them a quick agenda of a few things you would like to discuss. This helps them to mentally prepare for the meeting and come better prepared to help you.

Your mentor team will offer you advice and direction toward your dreams. Everyone on your team may not agree, but a good team will ask the questions that help you recognize your blind spots. *You don't* know *what you don't know, until you don't know it.* Your team is not there to give you a guaranteed course to make you successful. At the end of the day, you must make your own choices.

Best known for her talk show *The Oprah Winfrey Show*, Oprah Winfrey was mentored by celebrated author and poet, the late Maya Angelou. "She was there for me always, guiding me through some of the most important years of my life." Winfrey said in a Facebook post. In an interview on WCVB-TV 5 News, she stated, "I think mentors are important, and I don't think anybody makes it in the world without some form of mentorship."

Former Apple Inc. CEO, the late Steve Jobs, served as a mentor to Facebook CEO Mark Zuckerberg. The two developed a relationship in the early days of Facebook and often met to discuss the best business and management practices for the company. When Jobs passed away in the fall of 2011, Zuckerberg posted on his Facebook page: "Steve, thank you for being a mentor and a friend. Thanks for showing that what you build can change the world. I will miss you."

Former Super Bowl champion Darrell Green was mentored by his middle school football coach. Green said, "I had a coach who in a different way encouraged me that I could be a great running athlete. He was always encouraging me to participate, and I did.

And so, I think he helped me to identify the possibilities, which—I never even thought about."

Mother Teresa committed her life to helping others and was recognized as one of the most admirable people of the twentieth century, operating orphanages, AIDS hospices, and other charities worldwide. She led a remarkable and revered life, but she might not have achieved all that she did if it weren't for her mentor, Father Michael van der Peet. The two met while waiting for a bus in Rome, and quickly developed a close friendship. They spoke regularly and confided in each other over the years.

The stories of how those who changed the world all had mentors in their lives are endless. They assembled an advisory team around them to achieve success. The slowest way to the top or to your dream is by yourself. We ask for help not because we are weak, but because we want to remain strong. When I am working with someone, the first question I ask is, "Who else is on your team?"

Call You on Your "Stuff"

WE NEED PEOPLE in our lives who hold us accountable and call us on our "stuff." Those are people who believe in our dream and are willing to give us honest feedback. It may be feedback we don't want to hear, but we *need* to hear it. You can't see the picture when you're in the frame. We all have blind spots that we need other people to point out, if we are going to take our life to the next level.

I try to make a couple of videos a week for my YouTube channel. I remember when I first started, I made about 70 videos over a couple months' period. I was excited about my progress. I knew they were not perfect, but many people expressed to me that they were enjoying them, so I became complacent in the quality of the message and the editing.

I was having dinner with a friend whom I had not seen in a long time. I was excited to talk about my videos. During dinner, I casually brought up the videos and asked if he had watched any. He said, "Yes, but they are not very good. If I was hiring a speaker, I would not hire you based on your videos." He continued, "I have seen you speak in front of audiences; you know how to inspire a crowd, but the videos do not show your charisma." Wow! I was stunned. I didn't want to hear his feedback, but I needed to hear it. I was appreciative that he was honest with me.

The feedback I received from my friend was invaluable because when I looked at the videos through a different lens, he was right. They were kind of flat. They didn't show my sense of humor, or the energy that I have on stage in front of an audience. The feedback allowed me to make adjustments and produce a much better product for my online audience.

Be open and don't judge the feedback; it's there to help you. Don't let your ego get in the way of what you need to hear. EGO stands for *edging God out*. Don't be a wimp; learn to receive "gloves-off" feedback. The "gloves-on," sugar-coated feedback will not inspire you to take the corrective actions you will need to reach your dreams. I had to swallow my pride, but we all need people who will be straight with us because they love us and believe in us. A good accountability partner breaks you out of your comfort zone. There will always be people around to comfort you, but a good mentor is one who encourages you to keep improving and pushes you into new experiences. We don't get better by hanging around people who constantly tell us how great we are.

Thoughtful feedback helps you grow both personally and professionally, becoming accountable. It's a gift that people who care about your personal and professional success can provide. But they'll only provide feedback if you are approachable and allow them to feel comfortable giving you the feedback. Show your appreciation to the person providing the feedback. They'll feel encouraged and will want to keep helping and supporting you. The word feedback is usually associated with negative thoughts, because the only time most people receive it is when they screw up, or during annual reviews when they are told how they need to improve. Think of feedback as a positive experience. I have mentally turned feedback into something I look forward to. In my mind, the people I have enlisted to be on my dream team are holding me accountable and are feeding me information that I need to hear, because they have my back and believe in me.

Networking

"IT ISN'T WHAT you know, it's *who* you know" is a popular phrase that's been around for years. And you know what? It's true. I'm going to add to the phrase: "It isn't what you know, it's *who* you know, and do they know how you can be of service to them?" It isn't good enough to just know people. They must know how you can help them or their organization.

We all know people who have received a bonus or promotion because they knew people in the right places. You can either sit in the bleachers, yell, scream, and watch the game, or you can get on the court and *play* the game. It's called networking, and it's critical to the success of your dreams because it puts you *in* the game. I know many people who are smart, in fact very smart, in their jobs—but they are having trouble progressing in their career, because no one knows who they are or what they can do.

You may not like the idea of networking, but the reality is that having a vast network drastically tips the scales in your favor. Although education and credentials are still highly valued, most jobs never get posted to the public. If a job opening comes up, the first thing a company will do is ask, "Who do you know?" or "Do we have someone who can do this?"

First impressions are lasting impressions, so when you meet someone, give a firm handshake, look them in the eye, use their name or title, smile, and appear confident. Your networking starts as soon as you meet someone.

You should always be prepared to answer, in one to three sentences, what projects you are working on that will add value to an organization. When I was coming up through the ranks of the corporate world, my superiors would see me in the hallway or lunchroom and ask how I was doing. I never wasted the opportunity by just saying, "I'm doing OK." I would inform them of a project I was working on or an exciting idea I had that would move the company forward.

You will want to be able to explain your value in less than one minute. This is often called an elevator pitch. The idea is that if you met someone on an elevator and they asked what you do for a living, you should be able to explain succinctly what you do that will be of value to them, because they may be a potential client. For example, if someone asks what I do, I may say, "I help people disrupt their thinking and inspire them to live the life they love." That will always prompt their second question, "How?" Their curiosity buys me more time to engage in further conversation. If I were to say, "I'm a motivational speaker and instructor," they probably would not follow up with a next question.

Another technique I have used to build my networking and circle of influence is to use what I call the 5/10 technique. Select five people you know who you think can add value or influence to your goals. Consider those five people your major league team. Send them something to add value to their life or business once a month. It may be an online article, a TED video, an idea, a book. It really doesn't matter what it is; just send them something once a month.

One of my major league participants is a senior vice president of a security technology company. I send him articles on security, or maybe something about a competitor. Sometimes it isn't about his expertise, but instead just something about business or leadership. By serving and thinking of him, I know he will want to help me if I should ask.

Then think of ten other people who may have some influence to help you with your goals. This group will be the minor league team. Use the same concept as the major league participants, but send them something every three months. If someone on your major league team drops off, you can promote someone from the minor league. I have used this concept successfully for the past 20 years to build my network.

Networking can be awkward, time consuming, and extremely uncomfortable. However, networking is an essential part of advancing your career. *Your network will determine your net worth.* It's not enough these days to keep your head down and produce great work. You need to connect with others, express your goals, and build relationships.

R = Reinvention

"Life isn't about finding yourself. Life is about creating yourself."

—George Bernard Shaw

Time Is Now

TO GO WHERE you want to go and do what you want to do, you must be willing to let who you are now die, to allow for the birth of who you must become. If you died today, what voice, what song, what idea, what passions would you take with you to the grave? We all have an expiration date; we just don't know when it is. Every second of every day someone is born, and someone is departing.

Myles Munroe said the richest place in the world is the cemetery. You'll find dreams unfulfilled, music never written, ideas never pursued... People just gave up. What do you have—that if you don't do it, bring it, perform it, speak it, or teach it—that we will all be deprived of when you die?

Your time is *now*! You cannot wait any longer to reinvent yourself to live your dreams. People love to add two more days to the calendar: *one day* and *someday*. They constantly think about what they would like to do, but feel trapped in the life they are living. They think they will do what they have been wanting to do when their kids move out, when they retire, have more money... The list is endless as to why people are waiting for one day and someday, but the truth is, those two days never appear for most people. It seems we are more excited about the *idea* of doing something than the act of actually doing what it takes.

Start doing something, even if you do it badly. Anything worth doing is worth doing badly at first, if you are going to learn from the experience, and it gets you closer to your dream. You must get a sense of urgency. Your dream is trapped in your head. It's time to unleash what you have been thinking. Follow your dreams *now;* there is no better time. If not now, you will keep finding excuses to avoid becoming the real you.

My sister, who passed away in August of 2017 and to whom this book is dedicated, was also a beautiful woman with a special soul. She loved to laugh and dream, much like I do. There was a period when we would talk daily about the theories we had, discussing our next big idea or invention that could revolutionize the world. We were convinced that one day, we would be on the TV show *Shark Tank* pitching our big idea for the investors. I'm sure she is still coming up with ideas; but unfortunately, she will not have a chance to implement them. It was through grieving the loss of her and missing her that I realized I can't wait until one day or someday to live my dreams. Her spirit inspires me every day to reinvent myself and take myself to a higher level than I was the day before. I am now pursuing my dreams for the both of us. Jim Rohn said, "When the end comes, let it find you conquering a new mountain, not sliding down an old one."

There was a woman who liked to go running. Every time she passed by her neighbor's house, the dog would howl, "AwooOOO oo...awooOOOoo!" One day, the lady had enough courage to go up to the dog's owner, who was sitting on the front porch, and ask, "Why does he always howl?" The old man tilted back his hat and said, "That's an easy question to answer, Ma'am. The dog is always howling because he is laying on a rusty nail." The woman was shocked and asked, "Well, why doesn't the dog move?" The old man replied, "I guess it's not poking him enough to get off the nail."

What's your rusty nail that's poking you, but not enough to cause you to reinvent yourself and do something about it? All of us have nails in our lives that are poking us. Some of us have career nails, others have relationship nails, and many have financial nails that represent our unfulfilled dreams: dreams that we really want to pursue, but we aren't doing so for some reason. We all have dreams that we have been thinking about for awhile but haven't acted on yet. We are scared that these dreams will go unfilled, and then one day we'll realize it's too late; we missed the opportunity. Rather than take action, most of the time we just sit and howl. That's because the pokes by our nails aren't quite painful enough to motivate us. Wake up and know that your time is now!

Three Tiers

IT'S MY OBSERVATION that people generally fit into one of three categories. The top 20% of people are the "positives" in life. They get it. They are constantly practicing the techniques in this book and other books and are trying to improve every day. The middle 60% are the regular folks. They will say they are happy, probably live in the middle-class income bracket, and would like to move forward with their lives but are in the "wait and see" mode, or they have not found a way to win yet. The bottom 20% are struggling when it comes to moving forward in their lives and they're not willing to take responsibility. Unfortunately, these individuals are usually dealing with something significant in their lives that is holding them back.

Through personal experience, I believe the best place to be is in the upper 20% or bottom 20%, but definitely not in the middle 60% tier. The top tier people are obviously working on the right things. These individuals are constantly reinventing themselves, have a great attitude, and feed their minds every day with a vision of positive outcomes. They want to perfect the art of success, and they realize they need to recharge every day. They don't look for the problems in their lives, because their time is consumed by looking for solutions. It's a good place to be, in the top tier. You must be mentally fit to get to the top tier and stay there.

The bottom tier is also a good place to be, but those people who are there might not know right now why it's a blessing. Unfortunately, many people don't change or take action unless they hit rock bottom and are forced to change. Those who are in the bottom tier are either crashing or close to crashing, which will force a change for the better. If you are in this tier, it's not the end of the world; you will recover once you start making better choices and improve your mindset. Winston Churchill said, "If you're going through hell, keep going."

I speak from experience. The reason I wrote this book is because I was in the bottom tier many years ago and applied the principles I'm sharing with you to climb back to the top. The bottom tier can be a dangerous place if you are not willing to change your mindset. If you are in the bottom tier, I recommend seeking help from a professional; seek advice from a mentor or life coach. We all need help in our lives. Seeking help is a sign of strength, not weakness.

The other day I saw a guy I knew who'd lost forty pounds. He looked great, and I asked the usual question of how he lost the weight. He said that his feet went numb and he went to the doctor. After going through several tests, the doctor told him he had diabetes, and that was causing the loss of feeling in his feet. My friend told me he used to drink soda all day, and he consumed other sugary products without thinking about his health. He was forced to change because he hit bottom with his health, but now, he looks awesome.

Some people hit rock bottom due to a divorce and are forced to evaluate their values, goals, attitude, or direction in life. Others may reach a financial crisis in their life that forces them to do things differently with their money than they did in the past. The point is that it feels awful to be in the bottom tier. It's a lonely place. The good news is that when you hit bottom, you will be forced to change for the better.

The middle tier can be the most dangerous place to end up. People in the middle tier are usually conformers and have a little more than enough; therefore, there is no urgency to make changes in their life. Since life really isn't that bad, they don't take action to make improvements. As a result, they become complacent instead of chasing their passions and designing their life. Complacency acts as the brakes to your life. Complacency is like being in quicksand. You realize you're stuck, living life by going through the motions, but you don't really know how to get unstuck.

In one of my seminars I had a gentleman challenge me. He believed that there is nothing wrong with being part of the middle 60%, and insisted many people are happy in the middle tier. Challenge is a nice word; actually, he was very irate that I had the nerve to say the middle tier can be a challenging place where most people get stuck.

After the seminar, I thought for the next several days about the man's comments. I reflected on these questions: Is it possible to be happy living in the middle tier, being a conformer? What *is* happiness? Are those who say they are happy in the middle tier being truthful with themselves? It made me challenge my own thinking, which led me down many paths as I examined what I believe to be the truth about this.

I do think you can be happy in the middle tier. However, I also believe those same people leave a lot on the table in life. They will regret not trying something, or wish they would have tried something, or changed something along the way to increase their happiness. Fast forward thirty, forty, fifty years, when they are sitting in their rocking chairs reflecting on life. They will think phrases such as: *I wish I would have...* or *If I could do it over again, I would...* They will have more OK days than good days, while the upper 20% tier will have more good days than OK days.

I think middle tier people are coasters in life. It's like riding a bike; it's fun to sit back and coast down a big hill, without having to pedal. But if you want to get somewhere, you will eventually have to pedal, or you will be stuck at the bottom of the hill. The middle tier people may be happy in life and enjoy coasting, but at some point, a hill will appear. If you're not ready to start pedaling, you will lose your balance and life will push you off the bike. As humans, we work best when we continually challenge ourselves to improve, learn, and achieve.

Middle Tier

LET'S EXPLORE THE middle tier a bit deeper, since that's where most people live. People in the middle tier often confuse being happy with being satisfied, but there's a big difference. I'm not a psychologist; I don't know your life. If you are happy, I'm not out to change your mind—as long as you are being truthful with *yourself*. I stress that because I find that being truthful with ourselves is the hardest thing to do in life. Are you saying you're happy because you truly are? Or do you fear the change required to be truly happy?

Allow me to give you an example using relationships. I have found through my coaching that people sometimes confuse being satisfied or comfortable with being happy in long-term relationships. Is the relationship exciting, or just comfortable? Are you truly happy, or do you fear the change necessary to start something new? Some relationships become complacent, partners falling into a routine. Then, after many years, those people don't feel a strong connection with their partner but lack the energy to either improve or make a change. The difference between happy and satisfied may seem small, but it's a world of difference.

When you are happy in a relationship, you have passion. You can't wait to see your partner, and you're willing to make changes to make your partner happy. When you're comfortable, that feeling of safety is akin to that of boredom. The feeling isn't draining, and it isn't toxic. It's just vanilla: bland and homogenous, nothing special. Your motivation for staying in the relationship is certainly not your all-consuming, burning, and can't-live-without-it love. You just don't want to try something different that may require a great deal more energy, or you aren't willing to change. You're not precisely unhappy, but you're not joyous, either.

You simply exist in your relationship. The same is true with life and pursuing our dreams. Some people merely exist in their lives, and some people live their lives. Being comfortable or satisfied means you've talked yourself into thinking you really are happy, and you start to ignore the truth: that you wish you had the courage to take control of the situation. If you stay in the comfortable tier too long, you will slip into the bottom tier and become unhappy.

The difference between satisfied and happy applies beyond relationships; it also applies to what you do for a living. People who are happy are exhilarated by a new day; what they are about to do excites them. They welcome challenges and have the same passion on Monday morning as they do on Friday afternoons.

People who are comfortable in life have convinced themselves that it's too much effort to make career changes, so they might as well stay put, being comfortable, and make the best of it. After a time, these are the same people who wish they were doing anything but what they are supposed to do. They only do the minimum, watch the clock, lack new ideas, aren't willing to cooperate, and become secretive. After years of working in the comfortable tier, many will slip into the bottom tier of performers. The two biggest time wasters in life are being in the wrong job and being in the wrong relationship.

Where you fall within the tiers is not as important as being honest with yourself. If you are happy and you're being honest, great! If you are not happy, that's great too, because you can start working to reinvent yourself. I'm not convinced that being comfortable or satisfied is a fulfilling life. People who are just comfortable usually don't set goals that move their life forward. This is when midlife crises occur. We are happiest when we are contributing to our relationships, work, community, faith, friends, family and working on our goals. Those who are happiest contribute more and have active, meaningful engagement, as opposed to those who just go through the motions to get through every day.

Our bodies have three brains: one in our head that we use for logic, another in our chest that registers emotions, and the third in our stomach, where we have what are often called gut reactions. Our brains use a combination of logic and emotion to give us that gut feeling, intuition. If you ever want a clear answer to what tier you are in, listen to your gut feeling; it's usually the correct brain to consult when trying to answer difficult questions.

Our Beliefs

STOP, RIGHT NOW, and give your belief system a wakeup call. The reason most people are not living the life they love is because of their belief system. You must radically interrupt your belief system and your thinking. Nothing you have said, done, or experienced is helping you right now. Most people operate out of memory, not creativity. We must learn to live from our imaginations, not the past. Our most dominant thoughts are negative, and 80% of negative thinking by the subconscious mind goes undetected by the conscious mind. If you have a dream, you've probably already convinced yourself it isn't possible without noticing.

To achieve your dreams, you have to be in it to win it. You must be more creative, going beyond what you already have seen, done, and heard. More importantly, you must first believe in yourself. Every thought you have leads to an emotion, which is then tied to a belief, which creates your reality. We have positive and negative beliefs, but the most damaging of all beliefs is a *self-limiting* belief.

Somewhere, someplace, somehow, someone may have told you that we were not good enough in some way—not smart enough, not talented enough, not beautiful or handsome enough—*and you believed it*. If you believed whatever someone said negative about you or your dreams, whether it was true or not, then it became true for you.

On one shoulder, you have a positive belief system. This the belief system that gets you excited about your dreams and what you can accomplish. It's the belief system that pokes you in the side, trying to encourage you to live the life you love. On the other shoulder, you have the self-limiting beliefs that tell you that you are not good enough, don't have time, or are doomed to fail.

The issue is that the self-limiting belief on your shoulder has become enormous. You have been feeding the monster and watching it grow. Monsters don't live under your bed; they sit on your shoulder and reach into your mind with tenacious claws. For some, the monster is so big they are afraid of it. Whatever the monster wants or says, you believe and do. You may not like how big the monster has become, but for some reason, you keep feeding it with your self-doubt.

One of the things you must do to stop feeding the monster is to work on your inner dialogue. We are always talking to ourselves.

You can't help it; even when you try to have a clear mind, your inner dialogue is in chatting mode non-stop. You can't always control your inner dialogue, but you *can* control what you choose to believe and own. Sometimes you must stand up to your inner voice and say, "Shut. *Up*. I'm not going to listen to you anymore. I'm not going to let you tell me I can't do it, or that I'm not good enough." You must fight the negative dialogue that is holding you back from living the life you love and starve the monster. If you don't, you will spend more time living your fears than living your dreams.

Be careful of hurtful inner dialogue. People will say things to themselves that are far worse than what they would say to someone who has betrayed them. Some people have a hard time liking themselves, or even just being alone with themselves. If this sounds like you, you must stop this self-destructive inner dialogue.

You can encourage yourself by replacing negative dialogue with positive phrases, such as yes, I *can*; yes, I *will* do it; and I will *not* fear it anymore. One of the most asked questions you will answer in your life is: "How are you doing?" Start thinking of an answer that is not the standard "Good," or "OK." When I'm asked the question several times a day, my reply is, "Outstanding and getting better," or "I'm living the dream." Even if I don't really feel that way, by using strong, positive words, I am sending a positive signal to my brain that I want to feel outstanding—and as a result, my brain goes into motion helping me, supplying me with the right words and actions to feel outstanding. The same is true for the reverse. If you are asked several times in one day how you are doing and your answer is, "I'm OK," or "I've been better," chances are you are going to have tough day.

Be very selective of the words you think and use. Use strong, positive words that will inspire you towards action. As an example, change the word *should* to *must*. We always get what we *should* have in life, but you rarely get what you *must* have in life. Using the word *should* allows you to come up with reasons why you can't. When you use the word *must*, it sends a signal to your brain that what you want is urgent and non-negotiable.

Think for a moment about this hypothetical scenario: Let's say a family member, whom you love dearly, called you today and needed a few thousand dollars in a few days for a medical emergency. They called you because you are the only person they can count on, but you don't have the money to give them. Do you hang up the phone and say, "I *should* help them," or "I *must* help them?" I willing to bet you would say you *must* help them.

At that point, when you commit to using the word *must*, something changes. You would hang up the phone and immediately start thinking of how you could get a few thousand dollars. You would think of what you could sell, or maybe investigate withdrawing from a savings or retirement fund. You would ask your friends or visit every bank or lender in town until you got the money. I don't know how you would get the money, but I do know you would ultimately find a few thousand dollars for your family member. In a situation like this, you will not see any barriers. In fact, you will kick down every barrier that prevents you from getting the money, because failure to help your family member is not an option. When you reach that point of determination, you have grit.

Follow this simple rule: Don't say anything to yourself that you wouldn't say to anyone else. Throughout the day, stop and evaluate what you're thinking. If a negative thought enters your mind, evaluate it rationally and respond with affirmations of what is good about yourself.

The level of belief you have in yourself, along with your inner dialogue, will manifest itself inside you. Whatever you have in your life right now is because of what you believe subconsciously you deserve. The good news is, if you want more out of life, it all starts with you and your inner dialogue. You don't have to depend on anyone else to start taking your life to the next level.

Your Story

THE CONSCIOUS MIND can only hold one thought at a time. When you keep a positive affirmation in your mind, a negative one can't replace it *unless you allow it.* Study after study has proven that 98% of all negative self-limiting beliefs are not true. If you are not careful, your negative inner dialogue will turn into your story. You have a story because it protects you. The story allows you not to try as hard, or when you have a setback, you can refer to your story.

The problem is, the same story that protects you also imprisons you. When you have been telling yourself the same story loud enough and long enough, you tend to believe it. Small parts of your story may be true, but it isn't the real reason you can't reinvent yourself and live your dreams.

Many people are trying to lose weight, including myself. I had a story about why I couldn't exercise every day. My story started off like this: "I am struggling to exercise every day, because I don't have time." Sound familiar? I was using an excuse to make myself feel better, claiming I had no time to exercise. Now, you and I know that a lack of time is not the real reason I don't exercise every day. And if you are trying to lose weight, I'm willing to bet your story is something like mine. We can all find at least twenty minutes per day to exercise. By telling myself repeatedly that I don't have time, I convinced myself that I really didn't have the time. I got sucked into believing my own story.

We all have a story about everything in our lives. We have a story about our relationships, finances, education, position at work, and the goals we want to achieve. If you are in an unhappy relationship, I bet you have a story that you've told yourself for a long time, to convince yourself to stay. If you are financially struggling or having trouble advancing in your career, I'm sure there is a good story as to why.

Parts of someone's story may be true, but, it's never the entire truth; it is always the excuse. In my coaching sessions, I love to hear my clients' stories as to why they are not advancing their lives. Some stories are funny, some are surprising, and some are just plain hard to believe. I will be a good listener, even if it's a long story. My goal is to have them tell me their story for the last time. I want the story, the one that they've convinced themselves explains why they're not advancing or succeeding, to become a story of the past.

Maybe you went through an awful ending to a relationship, and during the breakup, the other person said nasty things to you. Now that they're long gone, you may be replaying their words over and over in your head, to the point you now believe what they've said and it has turned into your story. *Stop that!* Stop, right now, and change the dialogue in your head. Reverse the negative story you have believed for far too long, turning it into a positive affirmation. This is true for any area of your life where you may be struggling: Change your story, and you will change your outcome.

If you have a goal that you are struggling with, ask yourself what is holding you back. Listen carefully to the story you are telling yourself, then put your ego and pride aside. Ask yourself what the *real* reason is and see if your story changes. It takes courage to challenge your original story. Think of your story in the third person narrative; if you were hearing the story from someone else, what actions would you recommend they take?

Suck It Up, Buttercup

SUCK IT UP, buttercup—and stop complaining. I know, that's easier said than done. But it's vitally important that you don't complain to or blame others about your situation. You are not the product of your circumstances, but the product of your choices. Complaining and blaming is another way of making excuses, keeping you in the past and not helping you reinvent yourself to try new ways or ideas. Complaining makes you look weak. When you complain, you are advertising to those around you that you lack the creativity and intelligence to solve the problem. There is a difference between raising a point of concern and complaining. Being wise enough to see and point out potential pitfalls in any situation is just good sense. However, complaining about the same situation weakens your ability to fix it. Complainers see problems, whereas people with accountability see solutions.

I have worked with many people who want to change their situation but are not willing to change their thinking. They will blame you, me, their kids, spouse, boss, the dog. If you name it, they will blame it. Those people who want more out of life but are not willing to make changes live in victimhood. I talk to people every day who live in victimhood, and believe me, they are recruiting every day; they want you to join them. Their force is strong. They want you to be part of their club. Victimhood is a great place to live; you don't have to take responsibility for anything, you depend on others to take care of you, and nothing is your fault.

Many people complain because they are desperate for attention. I don't know if a need for attention is an emotion, but let's pretend it is, for the purpose of this chapter. In my opinion, it's the number one emotion in humans. Some people need attention on a large stage and some only need it in small groups, maybe even one-on-one or in an intimate situation. Whatever it is, we all need some attention, and it sits at the top of the human emotional survival chain.

As a society, we have learned that by complaining we get attention. Since other people like to complain too, we easily meet our number one need in life—attention. Some people will complain so much that they eventually don't even know they are complaining anymore. To them, it's just part of their conversation.

I am willing to bet that when most couples get home from work, the typical conversation goes like this:

"Hi, how was your day?"

"Ugh, it was so long! I sat in a meeting most of the morning that was a complete waste of time, and my boss threw a last-minute project at me. And remember that coworker I told you I can't stand? Well, guess who I had to deal with all day? How was your day?"

At this point, they continue to stand in the kitchen and complain about their days. It feels good to them, because they are giving each other attention. But unfortunately, instead of giving each other healthy attention and positive thoughts, they take the easy road out and complain to fulfill their need for attention.

I have had the pleasure of traveling all over the world for business, and I'm used to having dinner alone. I don't mind; it allows me to relax and reflect upon my day. Often, I will overhear the conversations of people around me. The story is usually the same. They will order drinks, place their food order, and immediately start complaining about something or someone. It's funny to me how people will use complaining as a conversation starter.

In some odd way, complaining makes some people happy. Certain people are not happy unless they are miserable, so they look for things to complain about. I know a few people who can't start their day without complaining. Some think that the squeaky wheel gets the grease—meaning if they complain, they will get the attention they desire. Maybe we learn this from birth. When a baby cries, the parents give the baby attention. When a child cries because the parent doesn't buy them a toy, the parents give them attention. When a teenager can't use the car for the night, they act out and the parents give them attention. By the time we are adults, we have perfected the art of complaining or acting out to get attention.

If you are a complainer, *stop*. As tough as life can be sometimes, remember that there is always someone who has things worse than you. No matter how bad a day you are having, it's someone else's fairytale. Constant complaining about what is wrong in your life will keep you focused on the wrong, self-limiting reasons why you can't make the choice to change. The opposite is true as well. Focusing on what is right in your life will keep you focused on how to overcome difficult situations.

I remember a time of not agreeing with my boss. He and I were not on the same page about a critical project. I can't begin to express the stress I felt over the situation. I started to lose sleep, wasn't eating well, and lost motivation. The more I thought about our disagreement, the more stressed I became. I needed to vent to someone, or I was going to crack. I called my mentor at the time and he agreed to meet with me. I couldn't wait for our meeting, because if there was one person who would understand, I was sure it would be my mentor.

The day finally arrived and after exchanging pleasantries, I couldn't hold it in any longer. For the next several minutes, I rambled without taking a breath, complaining about my boss for several minutes. Then my mentor did the most amazing thing; after I was done venting he tilted his head, cracked a smile, and said nothing. He was totally silent. His responding by just looking at me was powerful. At that moment, I got it. His silence was his way of letting me know that by complaining, I was focusing on everything I could not control, instead of what I *could* control.

If you are a complainer, chances are you hang out with other people who like to complain. Complainers like to hang out with other complainers. It's the law of attraction. We like to hang out with likeminded people. (Birds of a feather flock together.) Try to break the cycle of complaining. It's hard to do! If someone followed you around all day and recorded your conversation, I'll bet you would be shocked by how much you complain. Only you can make the choice to complain less, starting today.

Some people will go throughout their day trying to find things to complain about, so they have something to say and can therefore feel relevant. I see this on Facebook all too often. If someone makes a mistake, even the smallest spelling or grammar error, others are quick to pounce on them. Some folks will look for something to complain about all day so they can post it on Facebook. The food was cold at the restaurant, the service was slow, the traffic was horrible, other drivers are going too fast, the product was not what they thought. The list goes on forever about why people love to complain. These are the same people who will look out a window at beautiful scenery and complain about the spots on the window.

Complaining will not help you reinvent yourself to live the life you love. If you catch yourself complaining, stop and ask yourself if it's a legitimate complaint; are you just joining the crowd of individuals who have become complacent in their lives? Complaining reinforces negative energy in your mind, and you will miss opportunities that are right in front of you. When you complain, you tune out people trying to give you correct answers. Your stress levels increase, your critical thinking slows down, and you become an unpleasant person.

As a challenge, try to go at least 24 hours without complaining. If you catch yourself complaining, start the clock over. See how many days it takes you to go one full day without complaining. When my coach gave me this challenge, I thought it was going to be easy. Well, I was surprised by how hard it was to go a full day without complaining about something. If you can make it 24 hours, aim for 48 hours; then try going for 72 hours. If you can make it three days without complaining, you are well on your way to reinventing yourself. Get your mind right, and your life will become right.

Goals

WHY DO MANY people prepare a grocery list before going to the store? Some answers might be that it saves time, it makes the trip more efficient (so they don't forget anything) and it saves money. All these reasons make sense. You may have other reasons to prepare a grocery list to go shopping. It's interesting to me that people spend more time planning their grocery list than they do planning their personal or professional life.

According to international best-selling author and expert on goal setting, Brian Tracey, only 5% of people have clear, written goals—and less than that refer to their goals on a daily or weekly basis. Setting goals makes you accountable and gives you a roadmap to achieving your dreams.

I know, *goals* is not a sexy word. People tend to roll their eyes when the word is mentioned. Many people have not been trained properly on goal setting or been shown the power it can have in their life. I'm not going to dive into the art of goal setting in this book, but I hope to stress the importance of goals in this chapter.

People often ask me to help them when they are frustrated that they didn't get a promotion at work, or did not reach a level in their life that they wanted. I will agree to help them, but before I do, I ask them to send me their goals so that I can determine where we need to make adjustments to get the train back on track. Their response is often silence, or they have a look like that of a deer caught in bright headlights. They don't have any goals. This is a major part of their problem, as to why they are not progressing. These are the same people who go home at the end of the day and say, "I don't understand why I'm not getting recognized. I work hard. I give my life to that place." People often confuse working hard with a sense of entitlement, thinking they should be moving forward in their personal or professional life. Maybe they are working hard, but how do they know they are putting their efforts in the right place without goals?

When you set goals, it gives you a target to shoot for, to *Hit Your Mark*! Without a target, I guarantee you will hit it 100% of the time. Goals keep you focused on what to do and how to spend your time. By setting sharp, clearly defined goals, you can measure and take pride in the achievement of those goals, and you'll see forward progress in what might previously have seemed to be a long, pointless grind. You will also raise your self-confidence as you recognize your own ability and competence in achieving the goals that you've set.

When you set goals, you turn on your Reticular Activating System (RAS). Your RAS is the size of the tip of your pinky finger, located at the core of the brain stem just above the spinal cord and below the thalamus and hypothalamus. This is the part of your brain that filters out unnecessary information, so the important stuff gets through. It lets the good thoughts through to continue to marinate in your brain, and keeps the unimportant, distracting thoughts out. The RAS is the reason you learn a new word and then start hearing it everywhere. It's why you can tune out a crowd of talking people, yet immediately snap to attention when someone says your name, or something that at least sounds like it. When your RAS knows what you want in life, it awakens your consciousness.

Let's do an exercise that will help me demonstrate the connection between goal setting and awakening your RAS. Look around the room for 15 seconds and memorize all objects that are the color black. Try to memorize what the object is and the location. Ready, set go!

Now, I want you to try and recall everything you saw that were the colors blue or green. Wait! I told you to focus on the color black, so why am I asking you about blue and green objects? When I told you to focus on the color black, you became aware of those objects that were black. At the same time, you filtered out any objects that were not black, because they weren't important to the goal of the exercise.

Let's say you were thinking about buying a Honda CRX, and researching the price, color, options, financing, etc. What would you notice driving to and from work every day? You would notice a Honda CRX seemingly everywhere you looked. You would think there was a hot sale somewhere that nobody told you about because so many people were driving the car you were thinking about. Your RAS was in tune with your goal of buying a Honda, and it was making you aware of all the CRXs on the road to assist you in your buying decision. You didn't tell your brain to only look for the type of car you are buying, but when your RAS knows what you want in life, it acts in your favor to present opportunities in your path.

Your brain generates about one thought per second, so at the end of the day, that's about eighty thousand thoughts. Without goals, your RAS doesn't know what to let through to the conscious brain and what thoughts to keep out. As a result, we feel exhausted at the end of the day because we have too many thoughts bouncing around in our heads. Your brain is like your computer. If you load your computer with a lot of junk, it will eventually slow down and stop working.

When you have clearly defined goals, your RAS will awaken your consciousness to start noticing things that you may have not noticed before. It will also draw the right things and the right people into your path to help you achieve your goals. If you want to learn how to play tennis, and you have clearly defined goals on how you are going to learn, you will start meeting people who play tennis. You will notice articles on the internet or in the newspaper about tennis. Don't look at it as a coincidence. Your RAS is working in your favor to help you achieve your goals.

When you write down a goal, think about what Mark Twain said: "Your goal should be so simple that a fourth grader can tell you if you have achieved it or not." Keep your goal simple and eliminate any doubt. You must also have a due date, to hold yourself accountable. After you write out your goal, write down 10–20 little goals, actionable items that will help you achieve your goal. Most people just have a bucket list of things they want to accomplish. Our brain does not know how to interpret a long list of *wants* in life. It's too broad and generic. If you only had 10 minutes today to work on your goals, do you have your goal broken down into actionable items so that you could make progress toward your goal in those 10 minutes? Or, do you spend 10 minutes thinking about your goals?

You must write down your goals. You have more nerve endings between the palm of your hand and your brain than any other part of your body. When you write down your goals, you send a message to your brain about what you want to achieve, which turns on your RAS. Another reason to write down your goals is so you can physically cross off your actionable items when you complete them. When you accomplish a small task toward your goal and cross it off, it releases dopamine in your brain. This chemical substance gives you a natural high and motivates you, providing momentum to keep going toward another accomplishment. Without momentum, it's easy to become complacent.

Your dream written down is called a goal and a goal broken down into actionable items is called a plan; a plan backed by determination will allow you to *Hit Your Mark*. Michelangelo said, "The greatest danger for most of us is not that our aim is too high and we miss it, but that it is too low and we reach it."

Harold Estes

I SERVED FIVE honorable years in the US Navy, stationed at Pearl Harbor in Hawaii. At the end of 1993, I decided to leave the service and try something else. I was introduced to Harold B. Estes, who quickly became my mentor and best friend. Harold was 74 at the time of our introduction, and I took to him like a duck takes to water.

Harold was a retired master chief in the Navy. After he retired, he had a second career selling life insurance. Harold helped get me a job selling life insurance at a company he worked for, and they put the two of us in the same small office. I wanted to be just like Harold. I used the same jokes he told and dressed just like him. One of the things he would say as he held the door for someone to walk through first was, "Go ahead, age before beauty." That always got a good laugh from everyone.

Harold use to wear golf knickers—the short baggy golf pants that end just below the knee—with argyle knee socks and saddle shoes. I'll never forget the day he gave me a couple pairs of his pants. We went across the street to Macy's and I bought a pair of saddle shoes. The office was in stitches that both of us were now dressing alike. I think of Harold just about every day, and what I remember the most was that he was a master goal setter. Unfortunately, I was too young to appreciate the power of goal setting at the time.

Harold had a challenge with his hands. They trembled badly, to the point that he could not write. He also had issues with his eyes that limited his vision. He never let either of those things get in the way of his dreams, goals, or sense of humor. In the beginning of 1994, on a day I remember clearly, Harold turned his chair towards me and announced that he had an idea. As always, I was intrigued with what he was about to say because Harold was a dreamer, much like myself.

Harold told me it bothered him that the battleship USS Missouri (Mighty Mo), which at the time was an inactive ship, was sitting in a shipyard in Bremerton Washington. It was on the fantail of the USS Missouri, September 2, 1945, that General Douglas MacArthur accepted Japan's surrender, thereby ending World War II. Harold was a WWII veteran and was determined to get the USS Missouri back to Pearl Harbor and turn it into a museum. As he told me his idea, I politely laughed; I thought this was just another one of Harold's big ideas. You might have laughed, too. How could a guy in his seventies who couldn't write and could hardly see raise millions of dollars and get approval from the brass in Washington D.C. to move a ship from one state to another and turn it into a museum?

Harold soon started the Missouri Memorial Foundation, and day after day, I would listen to him on the phone trying to raise money. The beginning did not go well; Harold would hang up the phone after being rejected, think for a moment, then dial the next person. I felt sorry for Harold, because I just *knew* he was setting himself up for disappointment.

Harold had a friend who was the director of a Goodwill store down the road from our office. This friend was willing to donate space for Harold to officially open the Missouri Memorial Foundation office. I drove Harold down to the Goodwill location, and we were shown an empty space the size of a walk-in closet. This space had a separate phone line from the general Goodwill number, so I hooked up an answering machine, Harold recorded a greeting, and that was the birth of the first official office for the Missouri coming to Pearl Harbor. I can't remember how many times I drove Harold to Goodwill to listen to the messages, but nobody was calling to show interest or donate money. This added to my belief that Harold was more of a dreamer than I'd thought.

I left the island a few months later, and unfortunately, I didn't keep in touch with Harold. Fast forward to the year 2000. I grabbed a sandwich on my home from work for dinner one day. I made myself comfortable on the couch, turned on the TV, and saw the Travel Channel was on. *Well, this is good sandwich-eating television,* I thought. The host said, "Stay tuned as we count down the ten greatest museums in the United States." I continued to eat my sandwich, and then there it was—coming in at number four, the USS Missouri Memorial. I stopped breathing for just a moment and nearly fell off the couch. I remember saying out loud, as if someone else was there to hear me, "He did it; he did it! Harold did it!" I felt like a proud dad whose son had just accomplished something amazing. I researched Harold's number and gave him a call to congratulate him. The conversation was brief, but it's a call I will treasure for a lifetime. Harold knew the power of goal setting.

Liability or Legacy

I WAS SPEAKING with Mr. Les Brown on the phone, and he shared a story with me about his daughter, Ona Brown. He was on the phone with her one day, and she told him that she had a minute to speak with him because she was stopped and waiting for a funeral procession to pass by. Then Ona said, "Oh, no." Mr. Brown thought something was wrong and he said, "Are you OK, Baby?" Ona responded, "Yes, Dad. I was just surprised, because there was only one car in the funeral procession. When I die, I want a big line of cars because that would mean I was able to help many people's lives." How many cars will be in your funeral procession? Some people leave liabilities when they die, and some leave a legacy.

A start to leaving your legacy is to realize that life is about serving something other than yourself. We live in a very "me-centric" society. If you listen carefully, you will hear many people who are self-absorbed in the land of me. The more you turn me into we, the more success you will have, and the more good things will come your way. Many people are tuned in to the radio station WIIFM, which stands for *what's in it for me?*" If you don't tune into a different station, there is a good chance other people will be tuning you out.

One of the ways to get into we mode is to find creative ways to contribute to the organization or company. Your company is paying you to do a job. But they are also hoping you will bring more to the job besides what you are expected to do. You merely have a job when you start asking questions such as, "How will this affect me?" or "What about me?"

The world is full of people looking for jobs, and that means at any given time, you are replaceable. There is not one example of a company that has suffered because they lost an employee, even if they lost their star employee. If you come to work with the mindset that what you do every day is part of something bigger than yourself, then you are harder to replace.

If you feel like you just have a job, then you need to take time to reconnect with the reasons you are getting a paycheck. People who can't find the reasons that what they do is bigger than themselves will develop tunnel vision. Tunnel vision usually leads to self-pity. But those who know what they do at work is strategic for the company or organization are more fulfilled. This is true with family, community, and religion.

Think of being a parent. Are you just a mother or father, or do you feel that the responsibility of raising a child is bigger than the title? You should ask yourself the same question about your job. For example, let's consider a receptionist who answers incoming calls for a company. If the receptionist thinks that all he or she does every day is answer calls—and therefore is convinced it's a miserable job—is living in me mode. The same receptionist can change their way of thinking, reconnect the dots, and understand that their job is part of something bigger than themselves. A receptionist could see that, with every call, they can make a positive impact on someone's day with a positive greeting—and that they have a huge responsibility in transferring calls to the right place, which means happy customers. Happy customers lead to more revenue and more revenue leads to growth, which could open possibilities for advancement for the receptionist.

When we understand that life is bigger than us, and we serve others, then you will benefit from the law of reciprocity. The Law of Reciprocity is that that when you do something for someone, they will have a deep-rooted urge to do something nice in return.

Usually when someone reciprocates, it's far more generous than your original good deed. In fact, you should serve others, even though they may not be willing or don't have the resources to return the favor.

When you serve, you deserve. We were born to serve. I serve God, family, friends, co-workers, clients, community, etc. Imagine a world where people don't believe they were born to serve. It would be utter chaos. What makes western civilizations great is that as humans we understand it's not about us, but our ability to serve and be part of something bigger than ourselves. When we serve, we leave behind a legacy.

Dress for Success

MANY THINGS CAUSE me to be curious in life, and this topic is toward the top of the list. It amazes me how people who are in the process of climbing the ladder of success dress for work. Let's get something straight: It doesn't matter what the dress code is for your office or how your boss dresses. Ignore what you see and dress better than anyone else. Dress for success. I wasn't going to put this chapter in the book, but since we are on the topic of reinventing one's self, this is a great place to start.

First impressions are lasting impressions. Once someone has a first impression of you, it's burned in their mind. If it's a wrong impression, you must work extra hard to prove that their initial impression was wrong. First impressions are more heavily influenced by nonverbal cues than verbal cues. The way you dress is a nonverbal cue. In fact, studies have found that nonverbal cues have over four times the impact on the impression you make than anything you say.

Imagine that you are seeing a new doctor for a medical illness. If the doctor walks in the room looking disheveled, what would be your first impression? I bet you would be wondering if you should leave. The rumpled doctor must work harder to gain your confidence that they can help you.

If your place of work is casual, I'm not suggesting you wear a suit to work every day. You should always dress smartly. What is smart? I'll let you decide; I can't tell you everything. My biggest pet peeve with the way people dress is that sometimes their clothes look like they had an allergic reaction to an iron. You should invest in a $20 iron and iron your clothes.

For men, the shoes you wear will tell the most about you. In fact, it's what women remember the most about how a man dresses. Wear the wrong ones, and you'll telegraph a less-than-ideal message. If they look flimsy, a woman will suspect you're a cheapskate. If they're ratty and worn-down, she'll think you don't care about your appearance (and will wonder what else you don't care about). You can judge 90% of a stranger's personal characteristics just by looking at their shoes. Researchers at the University of Kansas found that people were able to correctly judge a stranger's age, gender, income, political affiliation, emotional and other important personality traits just by looking at the person's shoes. Men should have at least one pair of nice black shoes and one pair of brown. Throw some polish on those puppies once a week, and they will look great for a long time.

For women, there is a difference in dressing for work and going out on a Saturday night. If you have trouble walking in four-inch heels, you may need to wear two-inch heels. If you are constantly pulling down your dress or skirt, wear a longer dress or skirt.

Professor Karen Pine from the University of Hertfordshire studied the topic and wrote a book, *Mind What You Wear*. She found that you are what you dress, and that clothing has a significant effect on self-esteem and confidence. She claims clothing affects a person's mental processes and perceptions, and that ultimately, what you wear could let others discern how confident you *really* feel about yourself.

I believe wholeheartedly that you become what you wear. One of my first jobs out of the military was as a customer service representative for a new telecommunications company. We were a 24/7 call center with 70 representatives on the floor each shift. Although we never came face-to-face with a customer, the dress code was business casual. We were not allowed to wear jeans; most of the guys wore a tie, and the women wore dress slacks, skirts, or dresses.

Our clothing gave us confidence and a sense of being a professional who had a positive impact on the company—not just a call center representative. In fact, we won an award for outstanding customer service in the telecommunications field.

Please don't be confused by what Steve Jobs wore at Apple or Mark Zuckerberg wears at Facebook. I had a young man ask me in a training session if Steve Jobs and Mark Zuckerberg can wear jeans to work, why couldn't he? My reply was simple: "You are not Steve Jobs or Mark Zuckerberg."

Dress to impress. Ignore the studies that say that the way you dress has no bearing on how people judge you at work or your work performance. It may be true that if you're the best at your specialty and you produce great results, your boss may not care what you look like. The problem is that you will, at times, meet people who could help you succeed; you need to provide them with a good first impression. I tell the people I mentor, "If the big boss who doesn't really know you calls you down to their office to talk, would you be happy with what you are wearing?"

K = Kick-Butt Determination

"The difference between the impossible and the possible lies in a man's determination."

—Tommy Lasorda

100% or Nothing

YOU ARE LIVING the exact life you want to be living right now. That's right; let me say it again. *You are living the exact life you want to be living right now.* I repeat myself because it is significant for you to understand that you are living the exact life you have as if you had custom ordered it, because you did. The choices you have made up to this point have led you to exactly where you are. You have the job you want, the income you want, the relationship you want; you have everything you want right now.

Ready for some good news? You can change your situation at any time by making different choices. The definition of insanity is doing the same thing repeatedly and expecting a different result. You can go from where you are to where you want to be just by committing to do something different than what you have been doing. You are not the product of your circumstances; you are the product of your *choices*.

To accomplish something you have always wanted, you must

have fire in the belly—what I like to call grit. Grit is a measurement of how hungry and determined you are. A person who is determined will stick to what they want to achieve despite numerous issues, problems, setbacks, and failures. The United States Armed Forces has adopted a saying: "The difficult we do right away. The impossible takes a little longer."

Success requires 100% of you, not 99%. Giving only 99% to the effort is like saying, *I'll try*, and we both know the ending to the story. You might as well not even try if you are not fully committed. What percentage of your capabilities are you using now to achieve your goals? If the answer is not 100%, then we have some work to do.

You are not entitled to anything. It doesn't matter if you are a recent college graduate, someone who has been in their profession for twenty years, a subject matter expert, someone with a PhD, or you're just a nice person. I know a lot of people who think success will knock on their door because they are smart, gifted, talented, beautiful, or a good person. You and I both know success isn't just going to show up and knock. Achieving your dreams in not a passive event. You must have kick-butt determination and move with volume and velocity.

Success is a mental game. In fact, it's 80% mental and only 20% having the right mechanics. You must first be mentally determined to take your life to a level you have never experienced. When you are in the right mindset, your inner engine gets fired up and you become like an arrow flying straight to the bullseye of your target. Generally, nothing very good happens when we don't take the initiative to improve our lives. Successful people are not lucky; luck is when hard work meets opportunity. You did not wake up today to be average. You don't get in life what you want, you get in life who you are.

Determination puts the odds in your favor that you will live your dreams. Tommy Lasorda said, "The difference between the possible and the impossible lies in a person's determination." If you break down the word impossible, you get I-M-possible. Everything is possible if you are 100% determined. Kick-butt determination allows you to become better, to know better, to do better.

It's Going to Be Hard

ONE OF THE first choices you can make is choosing hard. It's going to be hard to *Hit Your Mark*. Easy is not an option. Winners know it's going to be hard. Winners know that no matter how bad it is or how bad it gets, they are going to make it. Winners have a willingness to stand alone at times with their ideas and thoughts, risking being laughed at, ridiculed, and doubted. You will often feel lonely with your thoughts. You will have self-doubt.

Going for your huge goals and being willing to be a nonconformer in life may even cause you to question your sanity. People will tell you to keep your secure, steady job instead of taking a risk and trying something new. They will want you to conform, to be like them. Yes, it's going to be hard. Success and failure are both hard; choose your hard.

What will get you through the hard parts is having kick-butt determination. When you are determined, you understand that there will be few problem-free moments. You must fight for what you want in life. If you don't fight for what you want in life, the things you *don't* want will surface. Many people fight for their limitations. Be warned that if you fight for your limitations, you just might be able to keep them.

You know it's going to be hard, so you will need to be self-motivated. People who lack self-motivation lack self-appreciation. This may come as a surprise to you, but neither I nor anyone else can motivate you. The truth is, only you can motivate yourself. Raymond Chandler and/or Lou Holtz said, "Ability is what you're capable of doing. Motivation determines what you do. Attitude determines how well you do it."

Just when you think you are determined and things are going well, life will show up and knock you down: new levels, new devils. Those challenges that we never see coming will test your will, determination, and strength. No test, no testimony. Your struggles don't have to become your standard.

I didn't anticipate my sister passing, or my cancer resurfacing two months later and needing a second surgery to deal with it. When things happen to you that you didn't expect, you can become bitter or better. I chose to get better. Our ability to handle life's challenges and remain optimistic is a measure of our strength and character.

You can never give up. Things are going to happen in your life that will turn your entire world upside down. Forest Gump said, "My mom always said life was like a box of chocolates; you never know what you're gonna get." It's at these times we must squeeze ourselves for every ounce of courage that we have in our bodies. An airplane only flies because of the resistance of the air over the wings.

No matter what situation you may be in right now, the simple fact that you're still here and still alive lets you know the world needs you. There is a reason for you still being alive. Eric Butterworth said, "Things may happen around you and things may happen to you, but only the things that really count are things that happen in you."

For true determination to occur, you must know your motives and refuel your motivation often. Otherwise, it's a short-term event that eventually disappears like a tiny puff of smoke. It can also have a disproportionately long-term negative effect, if we are not careful. Let's say you are motivated by a thought, but don't follow through. The lack of action can shine a spotlight on your failure, and then you feel even more demotivated.

Motivation is like using deodorant. You must put deodorant on every morning or you will stink. Motivation also needs to be used daily for it to work. It's a process, not a destination. I pride myself on being a positive thinker and being self-motivated—which is the best kind of motivation—but it's hard. To keep myself motivated and focused on my dreams, I refuel every day. In the morning I read positive affirmations to get my day started. I listen to something educational on my way to work. At night, I watch positive videos and study. Yes, being a nonconformer is hard. But it's worth it!

Patience Is a Virtue

WHILE YOU ARE determined in pursuing your dreams, you must also be consistent and patient. Consistent action yields consistent results. We live in a quick-fix society. We get frustrated if we must wait more than two minutes for service or sit a stop light waiting for it to change. We want instant solutions to every complex problem or fractured relationship. In short, we want it all, and right now!

Society has conditioned us to expect that everything needs to happen or come to us quickly. You can get dry cleaning done in a day, money instantly from an ATM, and a package delivered to the other side of the world overnight. When we are pursuing our dreams, we want them to happen fast. We think we can microwave our dreams and wants. Great ideas and dreams need time to marinate into greatness.

The story of the Chinese bamboo tree represents how patience and consistency can turn into greatness. I like how Matt Morris explains the Chinese bamboo tree (www.nattmorris.com).

The Chinese bamboo tree requires five years of nurturing—water, fertile soil, and sunshine—before it breaks ground and starts to grow. When it does start to grow, it will grow 90 feet in just six weeks. Did the Chinese bamboo tree take five years to grow, or just six weeks? The obvious answer is it took five years.

During the five years of nurturing the tree developed a strong unseen foundation to support the weight and height of the tree. The same principle is true for people who patiently pursue their dreams. With patience and consistency, people build strong character that will prepare them for adversity and the foundation to handle success.

Had the Chinese bamboo tree farmer dug up his little seed every year to see if it was growing, he would have stunted the Chinese bamboo tree's growth. The challenge is to stay focused and continue believing in what you are doing, even when you don't see immediate results. In a culture driven by instant gratification, this is our biggest challenge.

All of this requires one thing: faith. The growers of the Chinese bamboo tree have faith that if they keep watering and fertilizing the ground, the tree will break through. Well, you must have the same kind of faith in your bamboo tree. We get so excited about the idea that's been planted inside of us that we simply can't wait for it to blossom. Therefore, within days or weeks of the initial planting, we become discouraged and begin to second-guess ourselves—or worse, quit.

Sometimes, in our doubt, we dig up our seed and plant it elsewhere in hopes that it will quickly rise in more fertile ground. People change jobs every year or change organizations (and even spouses) in the pursuit of greener pastures. Often, these people are greatly disappointed when their Chinese bamboo tree doesn't grow any faster in the new location.

Other times, people will water the ground for a time, but quickly become discouraged. They start to wonder if it's worth all the effort. This is particularly true when they see their neighbors having success with other trees. They start to think about it too much. *What am I doing trying to grow a Chinese bamboo tree? If I had planted a lemon tree, I'd have a few lemons by now.* These are the people who return to their old jobs and their old ways. They walk away from their dream in exchange for a "sure thing."

So long as you keep watering and fertilizing your dream, it will come to fruition, just like the Chinese bamboo tree. It may take weeks, months, or even years, but eventually, the roots will take hold and your Chinese bamboo tree will grow. And when it does, it will grow in remarkable ways. You have a Chinese bamboo tree inside of you just waiting to break through. So keep watering and believing, and you too will be flying high before you know it.

Raise Your Standards

PEOPLE WHO ARE determined raise their standards and create great habits. You can look at a person's habits and determine what standard they have set for themselves in any area of their life. A person's beliefs show up in their habits. If you watch someone's eating and exercise habits, you can tell how they feel about their health. The same is true with someone's habits about their career, finances, relationships, and many other things, including the habits they have formed to pursue their greatness.

If you would like to create a habit to be wiser about your money, what are you doing to upgrade your skills in finance? Imagine your habits as three overlapping circles, and in the middle are the habits you are creating. The first circle is what you are trying to achieve. The second circle is your skill set. The third circle is a measurement of your desire and determination.

Determination is doing something even when you don't feel like doing it. Michael Jordan, one of the greatest basketball players ever to play the game, had a strong work ethic that he engaged every day. He had a routine that created a habit of working in the gym harder than anyone else. He said, "I hold myself to a higher standard than anyone else set for me. I'm not out there sweating for three hours every day just to find out what it feels like to sweat."

Building good habits can be difficult. That's especially true if you want to stick with them for the long term. Start with a habit that is so easy you can't say no. In fact, when starting to build good habits, a new behavior should be so easy that it's almost laughable. By the inch it's a cinch; by the yard it's hard. It's natural to want to make big, sweeping, drastic changes fast, but the goal of creating habits is doing something that will be *sustainable*. Little changes over a long period of time will create the habits that can be repeated day after day with confidence.

Want to build an exercise habit? Your goal should be to exercise for one minute today. Want to start a writing habit? Your goal is to write three sentences today. Want to create a healthy eating habit? Your goal is to eat one healthy meal this week. Want to experience the power of positive thinking? Make it a point today to think of one positive thing in your life. Want to be more determined? Follow through on one task you set out to do this week.

It doesn't matter if you start small, because there will be plenty of time to pick up the intensity later. You don't need to join a CrossFit gym and practically live there, write a book the size of *War and Peace*, or change your entire diet to super foods at the very beginning. To change your behavior and create a habit means you're adding something or subtracting something, and you must figure out what that is.

Ignore Your Doubters

YOU WILL HAVE doubters in your life; ignore them. There are those who no matter what you do, say, or dream, they will not understand. They will give you a thousand reasons why you can't do something instead of helping you build on the one reason something can be done. These people will stop you from achieving your greatness if you let them. They don't do it on purpose; most people are somewhat burnt out and have chosen to live a status-quo life. It's easier for them to bring you down to their level than lift themselves up to yours. Don't let other people's opinion of you become your reality.

I was speaking to someone close to me, telling them about my dream of being an international inspirational speaker and trainer. They looked at me like I had a horn growing out of my head. They asked, "Do you have a college degree? Have you ever been successful as an entrepreneur? Have you ever run a small business successfully in the past? Do you have startup funds?" To all those questions I answered, "NO!" Then they said, "I guess dreams are good, and you are dreaming right now." What they didn't understand is that I was not merely dreaming, but actively pursing my dream. I am consciously aware of my purpose and what I want to be doing. I was also aware that it was going to be hard. Don't let anyone tell you that you can't do something when they have never done it themselves.

What may surprise you is that the people who will doubt your great ideas the most may be the ones closest to you. When you start hitting your mark and living the life you love, it's your family members and best friends who may have the most negative initial reaction. Kick-butt determination is continuing with your dream when friends and family question you. However, it's important to understand their motives so that you don't misinterpret their initial doubt.

The people closest to you love you, so it may be confusing when they are not as excited about your dream as you are. One reason could be that they don't want to see you fail. They don't understand you are ready to fail forward, because that's the pathway to success. Some in your inner circle could become jealous that you have the courage to pursue your dream.

Another reason they may not support you is not as easy to first diagnose. People close to you love the way you are right now. They know how much time they get to spend with you, they like your personality as it is now, and they like how you think right now. They are concerned that if you do achieve your dreams, the relationship may change. The real reason those closest to you will usually doubt you the most has nothing to do with believing in your ability to make your dream come true. Their concern is that you might change, and as a result of your success, this may change the relationship.

Sometimes, your family and friends will support your dreams, but the experts may not. Experts could include those with expertise in the field in which you are trying to become highly accomplished, or those who have walked the path before you. You should always listen carefully to experts, but I have learned that experts can be wrong surprisingly often. Whether they are an expert or not, always remember to not let anyone turn you around.

Glenn Verniss

GLENN VERNISS CUNNINGHAM is a perfect example of not listening to the experts. He was an American distance runner and athlete considered by many to be the greatest American miler of all time. When Glenn was a young boy, he attended a little country school in Kansas that was heated by a coal stove. It was his job to show up early and light the stove to warm the classroom before the teacher and his classmates arrived.

Someone had accidentally put gasoline instead of kerosene in a can. On a cold morning in 1917, Glenn lit the stove and it exploded. Glenn's body was so badly burned that he barely survived; sadly, his brother Floyd died in the fire.

His burns were so severe the doctors told his mother he probably wouldn't survive. However, Glenn had grit; he survived. The doctors told his mother that he would have been better off not surviving, since he would be crippled the rest of his life due to both his legs being charred beyond recognition. In fact, the doctors recommended double amputation.

Eventually, Glenn was released from the hospital, bound to a wheelchair. Every day, his mother would massage his legs and feet. One morning she took Glenn outside in his wheelchair and he threw himself to the ground. He crawled to the fence and pulled himself up. He went stake by stake down the fence line, struggling for every inch. He wanted nothing more than to develop muscle in his legs.

Eventually, he started walking to and from school. He enjoyed his ability to walk once again and pushed himself to become a world class runner. He competed in both the 1932 and 1936 Summer Olympics. In the 1932 Olympics, he took 4th place in the 1500M, and in the 1936 Berlin Olympics, he took silver in the 1500M. In 1936, he set the world record in the 800M run. In 1938, he set a world record for the indoor mile run of 4:04.4. Glenn had determination; he was hungry to run again. It's a good thing Glenn ignored his doubters and the experts who told him he would never walk again.

Take Risks

AS RAY BRADBURY said, "You've got to jump off a cliff and build your wings on the way down." Taking risks is necessary to *Hit Your Mark*. Life begins at the edge of your comfort zone. It's easy to be determined when things are going well in your life. When your marriage is good, you're doing well in your career, your health is good, and the kids are behaving, it's easy to be determined. But at those same times, we can easily become complacent. You know there is more, but just don't know what or how to get going. Brian Tracey calls this the danger zone.

Dr. Johnnie Coleman tells a story in which a soldier was captured behind enemy lines. The captain of the enemy force gave the soldier a choice. He said, "You can either face death by firing squad or walk out that door across the room." The soldier asked, "What's behind the door across the room?" The captain replied, "All I can tell you is unknown horrors." The soldier selected death by firing squad and was executed. Later in the day, the captain's assistant asked him what was behind the door across the room. The captain said, "Freedom. But most people will select only what they know and not take the risks of the unknown."

To live your dreams, you will have to risk dealing with the unknown. Sometimes the word *risk* can sometimes take on a negative meaning. However, it doesn't mean skydiving without a parachute! You should take calculated risks. The very nature of risk means that we cannot predict in advance if things will turn out well. Just ask yourself, "Is it worth trying for?"

Most people do not want to take risks because of a fear or the loss of something, such as pride, money, friends, love, rejection, or failure. What you may fear or are afraid of putting at risk are the same things that could add great rewards to your life. For example, you must put your heart on the line to be in love. You will have to risk rejection to find someone, and then risk the possibility of heartbreak if the relationship doesn't work out. However, if you don't take the risk, you will never be in a meaningful, loving relationship.

If you are thinking about starting a small business, you will have to risk losing money and wasting time. However, it's those same things that you could gain. You could be financially successful with your business, resulting in giving you more time to spend with family and friends.

Taking risks takes guts. No guts no glory! When you take risks, it will stretch your mind and empower you to discover new limits, to go beyond what you thought you were capable of. Taking risks can cause you to become more creative. When you put yourself out on a limb with a no-excuse approach, your natural problem-solving skills kick in; you're open to new ideas and are willing to try something new.

Stop underestimating yourself. One of the reasons people struggle with taking risks is because they are not confident they will be able to handle the stress, responsibility, or pressure that comes along with it. You are capable of so much more than you give yourself credit for, so stop doubting your abilities! You can have more than what you have because you can become more than what you are.

Taking risks usually works in our favor, and we over-estimate the probability of something going wrong. As Daniel Kahneman wrote in *Thinking, Fast and Slow*, when assessing risk, potential losses tend to loom larger than potential gains. That is, we tend to focus more on what might go wrong—what we might lose or sacrifice—than what might go right. Because what we focus on tends to be magnified in our imaginations, it causes us to misjudge (and over-estimate) the likelihood of it occurring. Yet the reality is that the risk of something not working out is often not near as high as we estimate, and the odds of it working out well are often far better.

If you are not willing to take any risk, you cannot grow. If you cannot grow, you cannot be your best; if you cannot be your best, you cannot be happy; and if you cannot be happy, what else is there? In life we must get comfortable being uncomfortable. Get rid of these three needs: the need to be right, the need to be certain, and the need to be perfect. Jim Rohn said, "If you are not willing to risk the unusual, you will have to settle for the ordinary."

Failure

LEARN TO LOVE failure. You must fail forward and fail your way to success. Be proud to fail; FAIL stands for *f*irst *a*ttempt *i*n *l*earning. Sometimes we win and sometimes we learn, but we never lose. Falling down is not failure; failure is not getting back up. Les Brown says, "If you fall, fall on your back. If you can look up, you can get up."

The word *fail* has developed a negative connotation. If you failed to follow your parent's directions, you were punished. If you fail to follow the law, you get fined or go to court for a penalty. In a relationship, your significant other will tell you that you failed to see their side, which caused tension in the relationship. Many examples point to possible reasons why we think of the word *fail* as a stop sign, instead of guidelines.

The dictionary defines *fail* as the lack of success. I totally disagree with that definition, because failure is just part of the process of moving towards success. No one has achieved success without failing multiple times. Willie Jolley said, "A setback is a setup for a comeback." It's impossible to succeed without failing. Many people are afraid to take risks because they don't want to fail. You should want to fail today, because it will get you a step closer to your ultimate goal. You are going to make plenty of mistakes along the way, just like everyone else.

In fact, the most successful and famous people in the world have endured many failures in life; they've failed repeatedly. But when they were knocked down, they didn't *stay* down; they were able to get up and get back into the fight. They didn't throw in that proverbial towel. They didn't call it quits, or head for the ropes. They got up and kept going, and that's just what it takes to succeed. Some of the greatest gifts in life are wrapped in sandpaper.

If you've suffered through numerous failures in the past, or you're going through a torrent of failure right now, know this: failure will make you better, stronger, and smarter. It will allow you to reach new understandings and epiphanies on life, love, business, and the people all around you.

Oprah Winfrey was fired from a Baltimore news station and told she was not good enough for television. J.K. Rowling, the author who created Harry Potter, was a single mother fighting the depression of living off government assistance. She was turned down by all the major publishing companies. Now, she is the richest woman in the world. Thomas Edison, who created the lightbulb, said, "I have not failed. I just learned 10,000 ways that won't work." Michael Jordan was cut from his high school basketball team. Colonel Sanders was 65 years old and was not receiving enough money in his retirement check. He drove around to restaurants trying to sell his recipes. He was rejected over 1000 times before he started Kentucky Fried Chicken. Walt Disney was fired from his newspaper job in Missouri because he lacked creativity. His first business venture failed and he had to file bankruptcy, but he went on to create Mickey Mouse and win 59 Academy Awards.

Too many times when we have setbacks, we will label ourselves as failures. If you are guilty of this habit, *stop that immediately!* Don't let your struggles become your standards. Failure is an opportunity to learn. Let failure be your teacher, not your undertaker. You can avoid failure, however. Just say nothing, do nothing, and be nothing.

As human beings, we weren't made to merely survive; we were made to thrive. You need courage to be willing to fail. Winston Churchill said, "Courage is going from failure to failure without losing enthusiasm." We all have defining moments in our lives. We

HIT Your Mark & Live The Life You Love

all have a story that will challenge the reflection of the person in the mirror. Failure will never overtake you if your determination is strong enough to succeed. You must be willing to snatch victory from the jaws of defeat, and even if you can't, be willing to fight all the way into the belly.

187

Sacrifice

TO *Hit Your Mark* will take sacrifices. Sacrifice is not only a totally selfless act; it should also be viewed as a kind of investment, abandoning one thing for another of greater value. You will have to give up something to get something better. You might have to sacrifice time, stability, hobby, friends, sleep (but not for long periods of time) and yes, even your sanity, to some extent. Achieving your dreams is determined not by what you want to gain, but by what you are willing to give up: the amount you are willing to sacrifice.

If you want to lose weight, you might have to sacrifice eating certain foods or sacrifice 30 minutes of your evening for exercising. If you want to write a book, you might have to sacrifice spending time on Facebook or watching television to have the time to document your thoughts. Maybe you want to start a business and be an entrepreneur. You might have to sacrifice buying something fun for yourself to have money to take a class or attend a conference that will prepare you to be a business owner. Maybe you'll have to sacrifice spending so much time with your friends, or spend less time on your hobbies, to make time for what you want to achieve. If you want a job that pays better, you may have to sacrifice the stability in your current community and move to another town.

Advertisers tend to rely on this eternal law of sacrifice: "Lose your extra pounds without changing your diet, become rich without having to work hard, etc." We are bombarded with advertising that says you can grow your muscles without raising a dumbbell.

These messages reinforce the idea that we can reap rewards without making any sacrifices and promote the fantasy of getting everything we want without having to pay anything are extremely attractive. However, this is a false assumption all too present in our lives. There is an old saying: "If it was easy, everyone would be doing it."

When you make the commitment to achieve success and live your dreams, you are also making the commitment to sacrifice. Success is a simple measurement of the commitment and pain one endures to achieve their dreams.

In his book *Rich Dad Poor Dad*, Robert Kiyosaki recounts a common response he gets when he asks people why they aren't open to lucrative real estate investments. "When I speak to people about investing in real estate, they often tell me they're not interested in real estate because they don't want to fix toilets. When someone says, 'I don't want to fix toilets,' they're saying that little problems like toilets are more important than their financial freedom." For some, sacrificing their time to fix a leaky toilet is enough of a reason to never attempt to achieve their goals.

When I decided to start my own speaking, training, and coaching business, I knew I was also making the decision to sacrifice many comforts of life. When I came home from teaching or speaking I was often tired, but I knew that I had to study, design training programs, and write speeches for opportunities that I didn't have yet. But I knew that it's better to be prepared and not have an opportunity than to have an opportunity and not be prepared.

I also had to sacrifice some of my leisure activities. I took my vacation fund and invested it back into my business. I also knew that I had to spend less time with people whose company I enjoy. The list of what I had to sacrifice to start living my dreams is long. If you don't sacrifice for what you want, what you want will become the sacrifice.

The decision is up to you on how much you are willing to sacrifice. The bigger your dream, the more you will have to sacrifice.

I have worked with many people who had great ideas and detailed plans, but never acted because they were not willing to sacrifice. If you are hungry enough to live your dreams, you will make the choice to sacrifice. It won't be easy, and sometimes it will not be fun. If your dream is worth it, the sacrifices will be worth it.

Change

LEARN TO LIKE change, or you will like being irrelevant even less. The only thing constant and guaranteed in life is change. Those who live in a constant state of readiness are unfazed by change and step easily into what's next. They don't victimize themselves by wishing for different circumstances. They capitalize on change by having the foresight to be prepared for what's headed their way. Remember, success will depend on your ability and willingness to adapt, not on everything staying the same.

If you just remain the way you are, you'll always have what you got. Have the courage to make yourself available to new ideas and opportunity. When you know you need a change, or when it is forced upon you, have confidence that the right opportunity will evolve.

If you are willing to make changes, you can start improving your life immediately. If you are not willing to change, chances are the next five years will be like the last five. For things to change, *you* have to change. For things to be better, *you* have to be better. It's not what happens that determines your future, it's what you *do* with what happens.

Here is the good news: you already are a master at change. Take a moment and think of all the changes you have been through in life, and how well you did during those defining moments. Change helps us learn, grow, and reach new heights.

We like change when we think it's necessary, we volunteer, or we have a choice in the change. When change happens on our terms, we feel in control. Some examples might be deciding on our jobs, where we live, where to go to school, who we date, and what we buy.

We don't like change when it's unexpected, we feel it's unnecessary, or when it is mandatory and seems arbitrarily chosen for us. We feel a loss of control over the situation, especially if we feel we didn't have any input. A few of my clients have said to me that they don't like change. I would ask, "Are you married?" They would say, "Yes." I would then say, "Well, that was a mistake then, if you don't like change, because getting married involves change." I would then ask, "Do you have any children?" They would again reply, "Yes." I would continue by saying, "Well, that was probably your second biggest mistake, because having kids involves change." My replies usually invoked a chuckle from them, which served to emphasize my point.

Change in life allows us to stretch ourselves and grow. We don't need to like some of the changes that happen in our lives, but we need to accept them. Either you accept change or you will be changed. If not, life will feel like you are always swimming against the tide.

There are three stages to change. As strange as it may seem, the starting point for all change is an ending: having to leave the old behind. This is a challenge because we get comfortable with what we know, and to change means going toward something of uncertainty. During this stage, we have emotions such as shock, denial, anxiety, anger, frustration, and resistance. The second stage is the transition between the old and the new. This step feels like no man's land, because we have let go of the old and we've not yet adapted to the new. In this stage, we go from resistance to exploration. We start to absorb the change. Stage two can often be when we may feel at our low point. Stage three is when we start to adapt to the new and start a new beginning. Our emotions start to shift towards creativity, acceptance, hope, and enthusiasm. Change starts with the end and ends with the new.

Think of change the same way you did when you were a kid, getting ready to jump in the pool. You stuck your toe in the water and thought about how cold it was, questioning if you should jump in. Then you had to decide to jump in and the water didn't feel good. It felt *way* too cold. You question it briefly, thinking, *Should I get out? Why did I get in?* But then, anticipating what's ahead—the refreshing feeling of floating weightlessly in water—you hang in there, and are greatly rewarded. It feels good! Why? Did someone change the water, warm it up? No, you adjusted. With change, we must be willing to feel that initial discomfort, ride it out, and trust that we'll adjust.

Change in life can sometimes represent a mound of rubble. Some people have huge piles of rubble, representing a huge change they are dealing with, and others have small piles. No matter the size of rubble, I guarantee you there is a golden ring at the bottom that represents an opportunity. To find the ring, you will have to dig, using the tools of life mentioned in this book, and get your hands dirty. Change often is not a smooth process, but if you don't give up, you will be rewarded with new knowledge—and yes, also the golden ring.

In 1966, Richard Schulze, mortgaged his home and opened an audio equipment store named Sound of Music in Saint Paul. The company later expanded to nine stores, and a tornado destroyed one of his locations. Richard gathered his employees and said, "The tornado that destroyed our store has now given us an opportunity we would have never had." The tornado didn't destroy the warehouse where he kept inventory. He shared with his employees that they were going to use an entire year's marketing budget to advertise a warehouse sale and sell directly from the warehouse.

The sale was so successful that they repeated the idea the following year. Today, Richard Schulze has more than 2,000 Best Buy stores. The large retail chain would have never been an idea for Richard if he wasn't forced to deal with the change Mother Nature had dealt to him. Richard Schulze was determined to dig through the pile of rubble representing change to find his golden ring.

"When I was a young man, I wanted to change the world. I found it was difficult to change the world, so I tried to change my nation. When I found I couldn't change the nation, I began to focus on my town. I couldn't change the town and as an older man, I tried to change my family. Now, as an old man, I realize the only thing I can change is myself, and suddenly, I realize that if long ago I had changed myself, I could have made an impact on my family. My family and I could have made an impact on our town. Their impact could have changed the nation, and I could indeed have changed the world."

—Author: unknown monk around 1100 AD

Fear

THERE ARE MANY people living their fears instead of their dreams. There are hundreds of fears, but the main ones that keep us from our dreams are the fear of failure, rejection, success, humiliation, uncertainty, change, and the fear of missing out. Fear is an unpleasant emotion caused by the belief that someone or something is dangerous, likely to cause pain, or some type of threat. The issue is that most fears aren't real in the way you think they are. They're just a story you tell yourself, and you can choose to stop repeating it. A popular phrase about fear is that FEAR stands for *f*alse *e*vidence *a*ppearing *r*eal.

The irony is that these fears tend to become self-fulfilling prophecies. Research has shown a connection between the fear of failure and procrastination. That means that the more anxiety we feel about failing to reach our goals, the less likely we are to take action toward achieving them. It's a completely irrational reaction, but—as anyone who has experienced this kind of paralysis can tell you—it's a hard one to resist.

Any type of fear causes changes in the brain, as well as our behavior. Fear can cause us to hide, ignore, run away, or freeze, which leads to paralysis of thought or action. We may not always understand our fears; they sometimes don't make any sense. What we do know is that if we do not deal with our fears, they can hold us back from living our dreams.

I was speaking to a cafeteria worker who was explaining to me the good fortune she'd had making cookies after work and selling them in her neighborhood. She told me that every day, there was a line of people willing to buy her cookies. Her story was fascinating and one of inspiration. I asked if she had ever thought about starting a business to sell her baked goods. She shyly laughed and told me that while she thinks about it, it's probably out of her reach. I asked her if she has a fear of failure, since that's what holds most people back. Her answer back to me shocked me. She said, "I have a fear of success." Fear of success is sometimes more complex than fear of failure. On some level, it's more comfortable to stay in a familiar situation, even if it is not for our benefit. Achieving success means you are entering unfamiliar territory.

I have had a few fears over the years that have held me back. The standard advice people would give me never worked. People would tell me, "What doesn't kill you will make you stronger," or "Just suck it up and get over it." If you haven't walked in someone's shoes of fear, it's hard to understand how a particular fear can severely affect one's ability to deal with it. Tony Robbins said something in one of his videos that made sense to me. He said, "Sometimes you won't be able to eliminate your fear, but you just have to learn to dance with it."

If you have a fear to conquer, one tactic is to lean into your fear, not away from it. Leaning in means that whatever you fear, you'll do it over and over and over. When it comes to fear, you win or it wins. When you lean into your fear, you shrink it—desensitizing yourself by repeated exposure—and you win. When you lean away or ignore your fear, the fear gets bigger and it wins.

Another tactic is to fear something more than the fear itself. For example, maybe you have a side business to make extra money to send your child to college, but you have a fear of rejection. The fear of not being able to send your child to college outweighs the fear of being rejected. That will drive you to take action and overcome the fear. Also, remember your why of what you want to accomplish. When you know your why, you will assign it an emotion that will translate into the grit and determination you will need to conquer fear.

You can look at FEAR one of two ways: *f*orget *e*verything and *r*un or *f*ace *e*verything and *r*ise. If you have a fear, you must identify it. You can't change what you have not identified. Next, write down how your fear is helping you or holding you back. Last, write down how your life would be different without the fear. When you see your answers on a piece of paper, it allows you to identify, recognize, and make a plan for how to overcome your fear.

Final Thoughts

THE GREATEST GIFT you can ever give someone is the gift of your time, and you have given me your time by reading this book. And for that, I'm grateful. All of us are born unique, but most of us die copies because we conform. Make today the day you join me and become a nonconformer. When you *Hit Your Mark* and live the life you love, you will become the true you. Your life will become a representation of your energy, signature, and values. When you *Hit Your Mark*, you will be answering the call of life. Ask not what the meaning of life is, but what is the meaning of your life.

I hope in some way, somehow, my message reached a part of you that will inspire you to do something different. I hope I was able to introduce you to another part of yourself. You may not be able to change your destination overnight, but you can make the choice right now to change your direction.

Many people live as if they were a thermometer, always reacting to the terms and conditions set by other people. That is conforming.

You don't want to be a thermometer in your own life, you want to be the thermostat. Once you discover your purpose and know your why, then you can take control of the conditions. You switch from just existing in your life to designing your life. You set the terms and do not live your life according to the terms set by others.

As you go through life, think about the four main pillars in this book. Mastery is very important. Master something you love. To make it in this era that we're living in—at this major point in history, when things are changing at a rapid rate—you must conduct yourself above and beyond the standards that you've grown accustomed to in the past. You have to find something to master that you are passionate about, something that is *you* and that allows you to stand out as a result of your mastery. Expand, or be expendable. Be the master of your knowledge, skills, and abilities.

Surround yourself with accountability partners who are collaborative, achievement-driven, and supportive. Having relationships that will stretch you, that will challenge you, helps you grow. Associate with people whom you can learn from, people who foster your growth. It's important to have accountability partners to hold you accountable, pick you up when you fall, and be willing to call you on your "stuff."

The other step is to reinvent yourself on a continuous basis. Each day we must strive to hold ourselves to a higher standard. When you put yourself on that kind of track, it challenges you; it pushes you and stretches you. You will discover things about yourself that you didn't know. Constant reinvention means who we were yesterday dies to give birth to who we must become today. When you reinvent yourself, you set goals that cause you to reach beyond your comfort zone. To do something you have never done, you have to become a person you have never been. Robert Browning said, "Ah, but a man's reach should exceed his grasp, or what's a heaven for?"

It isn't going to be easy, but people who have kick-butt determination welcome the fact that it's going to be hard. Don't wish life was easier; wish you were better. Winners welcome hard. Everyone wants the good life, but not everyone is willing to work for it. You must have the commitment to do the things others won't do *today*, to have the life others only wish they had. Kick-butt determination is doing the things that are required, even when you don't feel like doing them, and having the perseverance not to give up. Be willing to fail; it's part of the process. Zig Ziglar says it best: "It's not how far you fall, but how high you bounce that counts."

The message of this entire book can be summed up with the words of Les Brown: "You have greatness in you. You have something special. You were born to win. You didn't come this far to only come this far. Life has no limitations, except the ones you make."

Your dream is calling you. It's time to answer the call. Today is not the day to delay. Whatever you are seeking, it is because it's seeking you. Now, what are you going to do with what you got? I look forward to seeing you at the top or from the top!

God bless! Live full, die empty!

Mark Jarema

About the Author

MARK JAREMA is an author, speaker, instructor and personal life coach. He has a passion for helping people disrupt their thinking, in order to help them take their lives to the next level. Through his career in the U.S. Navy, federal government, and as a business executive in Silicon Valley, he has developed a keen sense of what it takes to succeed. Incorporating his unique style, which is both entertaining and motivational, Mark has trained tens of thousands of people in over 20 countries.

Mark is a highly regarded speaker for the U.S. Intelligence Community. He has delivered motivational, behavioral style and leadership seminars to employees of the National Security Agency (NSA), Federal Bureau of Investigations (FBI), Central Intelligence Agency (CIA), Drug Enforcement Agency (DEA), Defense Intelligence Agency, (DIA), U.S. State Department and many others. For his work, Mark was awarded the Commandant Training Award by NSA's National Cryptologic School. Mark has also delivered trainings to 20% of the U.S. Fortune 500 companies.

Mark is a certified trainer and speaker for the John Maxwell Team and Les Brown Unlimited. He is author of the book *College Disconnect: Challenging America's Love Affair with Higher Education*. Born in Maryland, he treasures his time with friends, family and cheering for the Baltimore Orioles.

Website: **www.Jarema.Team**

YouTube channel at: **www.youtube.com/c/JaremaTeam**

Made in the USA
Middletown, DE
24 December 2019